Next Stop, Murder

by

Frank Semerano

New York Hollywood London Toronto

SAMUELFRENCH.COM

Copyright © 2008 by Frank Semerano

ALL RIGHTS RESERVED

CAUTION: Professionals and amateurs are hereby warned that *NEXT STOP, MURDER* is subject to a royalty. It is fully protected under the copyright laws of the United States of America, the British Commonwealth, including Canada, and all other countries of the Copyright Union. All rights, including professional, amateur, motion picture, recitation, lecturing, public reading, radio broadcasting, television and the rights of translation into foreign languages are strictly reserved. In its present form the play is dedicated to the reading public only.

The amateur live stage performance rights to *NEXT STOP, MURDER* are controlled exclusively by Samuel French, Inc., and royalty arrangements and licenses must be secured well in advance of presentation. PLEASE NOTE that amateur royalty fees are set upon application in accordance with your producing circumstances. When applying for a royalty quotation and license please give us the number of performances intended, dates of production, your seating capacity and admission fee. Royalties are payable one week before the opening performance of the play to Samuel French, Inc., at 45 W. 25th Street, New York, NY 10010.

Royalty of the required amount must be paid whether the play is presented for charity or gain and whether or not admission is charged.

Stock royalty quoted upon application to Samuel French, Inc.

For all other rights than those stipulated above, apply to: Samuel French, Inc., at 45 W. 25th Street, New York, NY 10010.

Particular emphasis is laid on the question of amateur or professional readings, permission and terms for which must be secured in writing from Samuel French, Inc.

Copying from this book in whole or in part is strictly forbidden by law, and the right of performance is not transferable.

Whenever the play is produced the following notice must appear on all programs, printing and advertising for the play: "Produced by special arrangement with Samuel French, Inc."

Due authorship credit must be given on all programs, printing and advertising for the play.

ISBN 978-0-573-66295-9   Printed in U.S.A.   #16128

No one shall commit or authorize any act or omission by which the copyright of, or the right to copyright, this play may be impaired.

No one shall make any changes in this play for the purpose of production.

Publication of this play does not imply availability for performance. Both amateurs and professionals considering a production are strongly advised in their own interests to apply to Samuel French, Inc., for written permission before starting rehearsals, advertising, or booking a theatre.

No part of this book may be reproduced, stored in a retrieval system, or transmitted in any form, by any means, now known or yet to be invented, including mechanical, electronic, photocopying, recording, videotaping, or otherwise, without the prior written permission of the publisher.

IMPORTANT BILLING AND CREDIT REQUIREMENTS

All producers of *NEXT STOP, MURDER* must give credit to the Author of the Play in all programs distributed in connection with performances of the Play, and in all instances in which the title of the Play appears for the purposes of advertising, publicizing or otherwise exploiting the Play and/or a production. The name of the Author *must* appear on a separate line on which no other name appears, immediately following the title and *must* appear in size of type not less than fifty percent of the size of the title type.

NEXT STOP, MURDER was first presented by Picture Films in association with the Gene Bua Acting for Life Theater in Burbank, California on April 14, 2006. The play was produced by Aura Figueiredo; directed by Aura Figueiredo; music by Clifford J. Tasner; production and stage managed by Julie Simpson and Erick Jonasson; set designed by Julie Simpson and Erick Jonasson; sound design by Tommy Francis; lighting design by Mary O'Sullivan; music performed by Dylan Gentile; choreographed by Paul Reid. The cast was as follows:

MYRON AMBERWORTH	Lon Haber
LILAH DAVENPORT	Kelsa Kinsly
TILLY PLUMMS	Michelle Ann Owens
DENA	Alison McMillan
FATHER	Marc Ian Sklar
KNUCKLES	Ian Madeira

CHARACTERS

MYRON AMBERWORTH: Professor of Paleontology
TILLY PLUMMS: His girlfriend
DENA: Teenage girl and leader of a gang called "The Scorpions"
KNUCKLES: Her cousin, and member of "The Scorpions"
THE FATHER: Dena's father
LILAH DAVENPORT: Reporter for a large metropolitan newspaper

SCENE

An urban city park late at night, and the lower to middle class apartments surrounding it.

TIME

No one particular moment but sometime during the nineteen-fifty's.

For Iris Huerta

ACT I

Scene 1

(SETTING: Bare. Black.)

(AT RISE: Spotlight on **LILAH DAVENPORT** *in a business suit. Her pace is slow and measured. She is holding a portable tape recorder. She walks forward and stops. A light comes on illuminating a* **MAN** *next to her. She makes her observation about him into the tape recorder. But he neither sees nor hears her. He fidgets slightly, looking uncomfortable, as if he is forced to stand in a police line-up.)*

LILAH. Myron Amberworth. 34 years of age, 5'11," 170 lbs. Recently layed-off professor of Comparative Paleontology. Youthful, mild in manner, hopelessly out of touch with contemporary life. As out-of-place in normal society as the petrified bones he carries around in his briefcase and pockets. Question: what does a man obsessed with things that are dead do when forced to share an apartment with things that are living?

(The lights dim on him, and **LILAH** *takes a few more steps and stops again. A light now illuminates* **TILLY**. *Again,* **TILLY** *neither sees nor hears the observations being made about her by* **LILAH** *with the portable tape recorder.)*

LILAH. Tilly Plumms. A beautiful woman who loves well, but not necessarily wisely. Because if Cupid ever needed glasses, or at least a reason not to show up for work, it was now. Because here, the object of Cupid's arrow is Myron – a small trophy in the best of times. But Myron's heart is an elusive target, having previously been pledged to all things old and residing in museums. But as Myron is a man apparently immune to her charms, she has decided that she cannot live without him. And perhaps that he cannot live without her.

(The lights dim on **TILLY**, *and come up again on* **DENA**. *Same business.)*

LILAH. Dena. A young tough and head of a small gang of ruffians known as the Scorpions. While other girls were playing with their Barbie dolls, Dena was out kidnapping them for ransom. She is a graduate of the school of hard knocks and her diploma is the small scar she wears with pride across her cheek. Where she lives survival is the game and the rules are any you can trick or force your opponents into following.

(The lights dim on **DENA**, *and come up again on* **KNUCKLES**. *Again, same business.)*

LILAH. Knuckles. Another member of the Scorpions. Personal ambition: None. Future Prospects: Zero. Life Expectancy: Let's just say there's no point in selling him any green bananas. What scares me is not Knuckles. It's the fact that I…I like him. He was young and trim, with a set of abs that had more speed bumps than a hospital zone.

(The lights dim on **KNUCKLES**, *and come up again on* **THE FATHER**. *And once more, same business.)*

LILAH. Dena's father. Tougher than the rivets he hammers into iron beams every back breaking day. But as the city he helps build rises all around him it threatens to block from view the very reason for his labors. Because every part of him is callused and leather worn except his heart, which beats only for his daughter. But he has trouble expressing affection, substituting instead carefully aimed blows to the ears. Not exactly a kiss on the forehead but actually preferable to one, at least in Dena's book, and frankly in mine too. Mugs like his are usually given away free with a fill-up at a gas station.

(The lights come up on **ALL** *of them, and* **LILAH** *stands back and surveys them.)*

LILAH. Nothing really out of the ordinary here. A typical tableau of greater metropolitan life. Except for one thing. One of them is a murderer. How do I know? I'm the one who was murdered. And that's not the kind of thing you forget.

(Blackout.)

End of Scene 1, Act I

Scene 2

*(**SETTING**: A park in the center of a large metropolis, skyscrapers looming in the background. Some benches, a drinking fountain and a few beat up trash cans represent the amenities. A few pieces of litter are strewn about.)*

*(**AT RISE**: It's late evening. **MYRON** is sitting on a bench with a tattered briefcase on one side of him and **TILLY** on the other side. She is happy and content, holding him in a fond embrace with her head gently resting upon his shoulder. He begins giggling softly and moving his feet in her direction. It is spring. He is young, she is beautiful and his eyes light up with some secret desire — one he cannot hide from her.)*

TILLY. *(seductively)* What are you thinking about?

*(**MYRON** playfully taps his foot against **TILLY**'s foot.)*

MYRON. Oh…it's silly. You don't want to know.

TILLY. *(snuggling closer to **MYRON**)* Yes I do. Tell me. We're alone…and adults.

MYRON. Well…right below my feet could lie a fossilized fragment of Cro-Magnon man. Yes! Proving the existence of a land bridge spanning the Atlantic before the Cenozoic period.

*(**MYRON** notices **TILLY** has stopped giggling is now scowling at him.)*

And…how unimportant it all seems when my nose is filled with the wonderful fragrance of your hair.

*(**MYRON** smells her hair and erupts into a coughing fit.)*

TILLY. Don't lie to me Myron! You're still in school. In front of your class lecturing to your students.

MYRON. Good Lord! You're right. I'm sorry, really I am. But think of what it would mean if it were true. What a discovery it would be. Even though Cro-Magnon man lived over 50,000 years ago he possessed a bigger brain than I do? Can you believe it?

TILLY. You don't have to convince me!

MYRON. It's just that professor Gibbons gets to mount expeditions overseas and I'm lucky if he mails me back a few sacks of bone fragments to examine. He's there and I'm stuck here.

TILLY. With me.

MYRON. Yeah. I mean no!

TILLY. *(Getting up)* I really don't understand you Myron. We're too different. Just too different if you prefer being with an old bag of bones to being with me.

MYRON. There is no difference.

TILLY. What?

MYRON. I mean between us. Listen my dear, I really want to marry you. More than anything.

TILLY. I'm beginning to doubt that you ever wanted to get married.

MYRON. Now don't start that. It's been a bad day for me. Everything that's happened…and now my poor leg.

TILLY. *(concerned)* What's wrong with your leg?

(**MYRON** *removes a fossilized bone from his briefcase.*)

MYRON. I don't get to keep it.

TILLY. Myron, why are you carrying that around with you?

MYRON. My last official act as a professor of this university is to take this to the museum. Once it was part of a rock. It took me one whole month to clean it. Poor guy. So long fella. Pal O'mine. Pete.

TILLY. Pete? Pete! Oh really Myron! How you do carry on.

MYRON. Yes dear. But three years of my life…

TILLY. Oh Myron, you mustn't worry about that now.

(*As* **TILLY** *gently kisses* **MYRON** *on the lips, a piercing scream can be heard offstage.*)

MYRON. What was that?

TILLY. Cherry lipstick. Do you like it?

MYRON. No, I mean the noise. Didn't you hear it?
TILLY. No.
MYRON. It came from over there.

(He stands up and walks past her, stepping on her toe and she screams.)

MYRON. There it is again! And it's getting closer!
TILLY. That was me. You just stepped on my toe. Myron, you're a bundle of nerves.

(Offstage the sound of trash cans being knocked over is heard.)

TILLY. Maybe…maybe we'd better leave.

*(They start to exit when their path is blocked by **DENA** and **KNUCKLES**, two young punks wearing black leather jackets with chrome studs.)*

MYRON. Let the girl go, she doesn't have anything you could want.
TILLY. Myron!
MYRON. I didn't mean it that way, Dear.
DENA. Clam up! Ok, Knuckles, they're yours.

*(**KNUCKLES** goes to the park bench and effortlessly rips out a slat waving it in front of **MYRON**. **MYRON** gently pushes **TILLY** to the side, keeping her out of harm's way.)*

KNUCKLES. Let's have the wallet, pops.
MYRON. I know what you're thinking. Typically nearsighted and possibly under nourished college professor, right? Easy mark, huh? But what you don't know is that teachers are like sharks. We both travel in schools. I click my fingers and you be surrounded by a faculty carrying so many degrees you'll think the temperature hit a 100. Think you can handle that kind of heat, bub?
DENA. Ain't nobody in this park but us, Dad.
MYRON. Really? Gee. They're usually out at this time taking their brisk evening constitutionals. Except for the ones

with asthma, of course.

KNUCKLES. The wallet pal. Now.

MYRON. You want my wallet? Sure.

> (**MYRON** *begins slowly backing up towards the park bench, keeping eye contact with* **KNUCKLES**, *who continues to approach* **MYRON** *waving the oak slat.*)

MYRON. No problem. There's a certificate of deposit in there too you can cash in.

> (**MYRON** *continues backing up towards the park bench.*)

But I should warn you, for early withdrawals…

> (**MYRON** *is now up against the park bench*).

…Certain penalties apply!

> (*In a flash,* **MYRON** *turns around and grabs a hold of one the slats on the park bench desperately trying to free it to use as a weapon. After much huffing and puffing he collapses on the bench unable to remove any of the slats from the bench. He tosses* **KNUCKLES** *his wallet.*)

MYRON. But if you wait thirty more days you get a free toaster.

> (**KNUCKLES** *tosses the wallet to* **DENA.**)

Look, you kids are young. Don't you see you're making a big mistake.

DENA. Let's see how good the legitimate world has been to you.

MYRON. 'Fraid you caught me at a bad time. But I wouldn't draw too many conclusions from that.

TILLY. He was fired last week.

MYRON. The term, dear, is layed-off.

DENA. (*looking through the wallet*) Twenty dollars! I'd been better off picking the pockets of a pool table.

MYRON. Who are you guys? There aren't supposed to be any gangs in this park.

KNUCKLES. We're the Scorpions.

(KNUCKLES turns around and points to an insignia on his vest.)

KNUCKLES. See that? That's a Scorpion.

TILLY. It looks like a lobster.

KNUCKLES. I don't care if it looks like a lobster, it's a scorpion!

TILLY. If you say so.

KNUCKLES. I say so!

DENA. Settle down, Knuckles. And now pop, the briefcase.

(KNUCKLES begins walking towards MYRON. once again carrying the oak slat.)

MYRON. My briefcase? Oh sure. No problem.

(MYRON begins to back up towards the park bench keeping eye contact with KNUCKLES.)

It's a nice briefcase. It was a gift. Made out of alligator.

(MYRON keeps slowly moving back towards the the park bench maintaining eye contact with KNUCKLES.)

Funny thing about alligators. Even when you think they're dead…

(MYRON is against the park bench again.)

…They can still come back to bite you!

(In a flash, MYRON turns around and tries once again to wrest free an oak slat from the park bench to use as a weapon and is once again unsuccessful. After much huffing and puffing, he collapses on the bench and tosses KNUCKLES his briefcase.)

MYRON. Oh here, hell, take it!

(KNUCKLES opens the briefcase and pulls out the fossilized bone.)

KNUCKLES. What the…

MYRON. Careful! It took me a month to finish that.

DENA. Uh huh. Hey, Knuckles, come over here.

(They both look at MYRON. His tie is being fixed and

straightened by **TILLY**, *who, fussing over him, is also wiping smudges off his face.* **KNUCKLES** *and* **DENA** *strain to overhear what they're saying.)*

MYRON. Darling, please!

TILLY. Really, Myron. You don't want to go through life looking like you've just been mugged.

MYRON. But we are being mugged!

*(***MYRON** *grabs an oak slat on the park bench and shakes it trying to loosen it again with no success.)*

TILLY. Myron, these children are barely old enough to knock over their own piggy banks. And frankly, the one with the lobster on his jacket looks like he might even have trouble doing that.

*(***DENA** *shoots* **KNUCKLES** *a disapproving look and he just shrugs his shoulders in response looking embarrassed.* **DENA** *reluctantly surrenders the bone and briefcase to* **MYRON.***)*

DENA. Uh, you can have your briefcase back. You can go now. And I'd get out of the park before it gets any later.

MYRON. Gee thanks, Officer!

*(***MYRON** *begins to reorganize the papers in his briefcase.)*

KNUCKLES. Com'on, let's get outta here!

KNUCKLES. Just a sec. So, what were you before you got canned, Pop?

MYRON. A professor of paleontology, if you must know. The study of ancient man.

DENA. Ancient man, huh? Now look pop, I'm going to do something I've never done before. I am going to put the twenty dollars back in your wallet.

*(***DENA** *hands him the wallet.* **MYRON** *looks upward and smiles broadly. However,* **TILLY.** *immediately takes the wallet, removes the $20 from it and hands it back to* **DENA.***)*

TILLY. Don't make me laugh!

MYRON. What happened to the twenty dollars?

TILLY. Myron has studied paleontology for twelve years.

DENA. The last twelve years, huh?

> (**DENA** *returns the twenty dollars to* **MYRON**. **TILLY.** *immediately takes it from him and hands it back to* **DENA** *again.*)

TILLY. He doesn't need your charity! His future is as bright as the stars above. With his education any faculty would be proud to hire him!

MYRON. Will you leave the twenty dollars alone!

DENA. All I know is with all that education he's out of a job.

MYRON. For your information I'd still have my job, thank you, if only more students had signed up for my class. Those ingrates! I offered them a chance to learn about the exciting world of comparative paleontology. Now they'll never know.

DENA. Yeah, the world's full of tragedies alright.

MYRON. To think, all I needed to keep my job was just two more students…two more students, hmmm…just two more students.

DENA. Gee, you sure got a funny look in your eyes, Pop. Like you was thinking…forget it!

MYRON. But why not? You'd love it.

DENA. Easy now. I know how to defend myself.

MYRON. So did Homo Erectus, who formed loose bands during the third glacier period around 500,000 years ago. Paleontology 101 is filled with facts just as interesting.

DENA. Knuckles, get him! Quick, before he puts me to sleep.

MYRON. But it's not just learning facts. No, we would take field trips to museums. Have access to valuable artifacts that the public never gets to see.

DENA. *(pause)* Access to valuable artifacts…that the public never gets to see?

MYRON. Hundreds of them! Still crated and locked in the museums basement.

DENA. *(shyly)* Could Knuckles and I get to sit together.

KNUCKLES. You crazy?

TILLY. And how!

MYRON & DENA. *(To each other and at the same time)* Excuse me.

(**MYRON** *takes* **TILLY** *to one end of the stage and* **DENA** *takes* **KNUCKLES** *to the other.*)

TILLY. You've got to be out of your mind! You're going to ask these delinquents to enroll in your class?

MYRON. You have to admit they're not exactly from the criminal mold. Not exactly. And if I don't get to the President of the college right now and tell him I've got enough students to start up my class I may not work again in this city.

KNUCKLES. You've got to be out of your mind! Your asking me to go back to school?

DENA. Didn't you hear what he said? We'd have access to valuable artifacts. One good heist from a museum and it's easy street for us. This may be our only chance. A museum basement full of treasure.

(The two groups meet again in the center of the stage.)

DENA. Well, we're in daddyo...er, I mean professor.

(**DENA** *takes the oak slat* **KNUCKLES.** *is holding and tosses it away.*)

MYRON. You won't regret it. It won't be easy. You'll be starting from the ground up.

KNUCKLES. I thought we was starting from the basement.

(**DENA** *hits* **KNUCKLES.**)

DENA. You know, we ain't been in a class for a long time. And then only in a high school.

MYRON. Oh college isn't so different from high school.

However, so we're all starting on the right foot, I'd like to have my money back. After all, we don't steal from our teachers.

KNUCKLES. I thought he said it wasn't going to be no different from high school.

DENA. Hand it over, Knuckles. There you go, Prof. We'll be at college bright and early Monday morning. Get the address, Knuckles.

(**KNUCKLES** *walks over to the park bench and effortlessly rips out an oak slat and walks up to* **MYRON**.)

KNUCKLES. Let's have the address, Dad.

MYRON. Er, um, uh, Dena...

(**DENA** *knocks out the stick out of* **KNUCKLES***'s hand*.)

DENA. Hey what are you doing? He's our friend now. He ain't holding out on us. He wants to give you the address!

MYRON. Say, Dena, he's not going to do a lot of that in class is he?

DENA. Nah. Now if I were you, I *really* would get out of this park before it gets any later. There are a lot of other gangs here and not many of them are as interested in good education as we are. I'll give you my jacket. Nobody messes with a Scorpion.

(**MYRON** *and* **TILLY** *begin to exit from the Park.* **MYRON** *stops for a second, looks at the park bench and kicks it, and yells as he hurts his foot.* **TILLY** *helps him hop off stage.*)

KNUCKLES. This is too much trouble. I still think we should have just kept the twenty dollars. What's in a museum anyway? I never been in a museum.

DENA. I been in one once. They keep a bunch of useless things in there that don't work anymore.

KNUCKLES. Gee, I hope I don't run into my father.

(*Blackout*.)

End of Scene 2, Act I

Scene 3

*(**SETTING:** A modest bachelor apartment. Somewhat messy but not excessively so. If the furnishings don't convey the fact the apartment is located in a low-rent district then the elevated train which rumbles by the window every so often should. Prominent fixtures are a couch, desk, and coffee table with a small TV on it. And a couple of dingy ornate wall-sconces made up of a number of candles and decorative crystals.)*

*(**AT RISE:** **DENA** is at the desk reading a book. **KNUCKLES** is lying on a couch tearing pages out of a book. He scrunches them up and tosses them in a wastepaper basket. A low glow can be been seen emanating from the TV – the back of it faces the audience. **LILAH** walks in-between them, unseen by them, and addresses the audience.)*

LILAH. Had Myron never enrolled these two kids in his class, we could all leave now and enjoy a cool one at Arnie's. Because you see at this time I was still alive. Enroute from Istanbul following a lead in a story. And this is the room where I finally met my own end. At least I got to know a lot of swell fellas who got to meet it first.

(After looking at her profile in the mirror, she walks towards the audience)

This is where a revolver was emptied into me. I thought I was good at avoiding danger, but I couldn't avoid the bullets that came at me faster than sailors at a waterfront bar. Guys - I could dodge. The six lead pills that put me on a permanent diet - I couldn't. In less than a week from now, I'd be found crumpled up on the floor right over there. With a cop bent gently over me trying to find a heartbeat. The only time a guy ever had his head against my chest just to see if I was ok. Of course the cops in Istanbul were always claiming to do the same thing. But I never believed them because they were always doing it after pulling me over for minor traffic violations.

(She looks closely at the spot on the floor where her body will soon lay.)

LILAH. *(cont'd)* All in all I should have stayed in Istanbul. Because soon I'd be walking through that front door not knowing the fate that was to await me.

(She exits.)

KNUCKLES. Hey, Dena, come here quick. The Martians are about to land and blow up the town. Gee, I hope they don't forget the school.

DENA. Keep it down. I'm busy with this book, ok.

KNUCKLES. Hey, like I ain't busy with mine?

*(**KNUCKLES** rips another page out of his book rolls it into a ball and tosses it in the wastepaper basket.)*

DENA. Turn down that TV. I'm trying to concentrate. I've got to find out exactly what's worth stealing, don't I? Hmmm…now here's a provocative chapter on Paleolithic Artifacts and their influence on Sub-Tropic Agrarian Societies.

KNUCKLES. I tell you I don't feel like I belong to one of the cities most feared gangs anymore.

DENA. Ok, ok, I know this has been rough on you, that's why I got you a little surprise. I was going to save it for later but…

*(**DENA** gets up from behind the desk and walks over to **KNUCKLES** and hands him a box. **KNUCKLES**, very excited, opens it, and pulls out a shoulder book bag made out of canvas.)*

KNUCKLES. A book bag?

DENA. What? It don't fit?

KNUCKLES. Oh I think I could get your head to fit inside it alright. And the rest of you with room to spare.

DENA. Should it to be my presumption then, that you are not happy with my gift?

KNUCKLES. Presumption! Provocative! I swear, being with you lately is like being sealed inside a can of alphabet soup that somebody keeps shaking up. I don't like this job! I don't like it!

(*There is a knock on the door.*)

DENA. Will you calm down! You've been making so much noise I bet it's the Super. Keep it down and put those papers in order.

(**DENA** *opens the door and* **MYRON** *walks in. He appears unkempt, as though he hasn't slept for a few days.*)

DENA. Professor! Say, you look terrible.

MYRON. Like I had trouble getting out of the park?

DENA. I can't believe any gang would mess with a guy wearing a scorpion jacket.

KNUCKLES. I can.

(**KNUCKLES** *continues to collate papers.*)

MYRON. Oh the gangs didn't give me any trouble. But the police don't think much of you. That jacket you gave me...the pockets contained 12 watches and 8 rings. Now isn't that odd?

KNUCKLES. No, not everybody who owns a watch wears a ring.

DENA. I think he means the cops thought he stole them.

MYRON. That's what I mean.

DENA. You didn't rat on us?

MYRON. Oh it was tempting, believe me it was tempting. But I really believed you promised to go straight.

DENA. We have professor, we have. Believe me.

(**MYRON** *sits down on a bench.*)

MYRON. I'd like to. But there is still one thing that's bothering me.

DENA. What's that professor?

(**MYRON** *jumps up angry and yells.*)

MYRON. What is a public park bench doing in my apartment!?

DENA. Well, it's not like you have a lot of chairs in here.

MYRON. I suppose I should be happy you didn't drag the park lamppost in here too.

(**MYRON**'s *eyes narrow as he walks over to an unfamiliar lighting fixture and slowly lifts the lamp shade. he quickly replaces it and shuts his eyes.* **DENA** *hands* **MYRON** *some envelopes.*)

DENA. Anyway, we saved your mail for you.

(**KNUCKLES** *walks over to* **MYRON** *and looks over his shoulder, at his mail.*)

KNUCKLES. There are a lot of pink envelopes in there addressed, "To the most handsome Man in the World."

(**KNUCKLES** *looks at* **MYRON** *closely.*)

You got a roommate?

MYRON. Those are from Tilly to me!

KNUCKLES. Nice girl.

DENA. Can I have my watches and rings back?

MYRON. The police are trying to return them to their rightful owners!

DENA. But one of them was actually mine.

MYRON. Why don't I feel bad?

(*The doorbell rings, and* **MYRON** *answers it. A large* **MAN** *is standing on the other side.*)

Hello.

(*The* **MAN** *brushes past* **MYRON** *and angrily approaches* **DENA.**)

THE FATHER. There you are! Where you been? I just noticed you were missing.

DENA. I've been gone three days and you just now noticed?

THE FATHER. Well the lawn ain't been cut, the garbage is piling up out back and the faucet still leaks. So I figured you was still around.

DENA. Oh that's cute, Dad, real cute!

THE FATHER. So what are you doing here?

DENA. I'm reading.

THE FATHER. You got to come over here to read? We ain't got the TV Guide back home?

DENA. I'm reading a book, a real book.

(**DENA** *holds up a book, and her* **FATHER** *takes it and opens it up.*)

THE FATHER. Oh really? Then maybe you can tell me what this word means?

(**DENA** *looks closely at the text.*)

DENA. What word?

THE FATHER. This word!

(*He slams the book shut on* **DENA**'s *nose.*)

DENA. Ouch! Hey Man, what's your problem?

THE FATHER. I ain't got no problem. No, I'm the richest man in the city. I can afford to take time off from work and get docked a days pay to go looking for my daughter! We're in the middle of building a bridge for Christ's sake!

(**DENA** *smells him.*)

DENA. What, over a river of beer?

(**THE FATHER** *hits* **DENA** *on the head with the book.*)

THE FATHER. Maybe you make your old man drink!

DENA. Yeah sure, and I make the sun go up and the flowers bloom.

THE FATHER. I never touched a drink until you were born.

DENA. Somebody had to teach you how to use a bottle-opener.

(**THE FATHER** *hits* **DENA** *on the head with the book again.*)

THE FATHER. Fresh kid! Why don't you go in the army like your brother. Do you remember your brother? You're never around when your brother comes home on leave. Remember what your brother looks like?

(**THE FATHER** *takes out his wallet and opens it up, showing* **DENA** *a family picture.*)

THE FATHER. Go on. Let's see if you remember what your brother looks like. Go on, pick out your brother.

(**DENA** *looks closely at the wallet.*)

DENA. Uhhh...

(**THE FATHER** *shuts the wallet closed on* **DENA**'s *nose.*)

THE FATHER. That's what your brother looks like!

DENA. Ouch! Hey man, will you lay off the nose!

THE FATHER. You're lucky it's only your nose. My father, God bless him, would have tied me to the back of his tractor and driven over a cactus patch if I talked back to him. He would have held my nose to a hot stove and beat the bottoms of my feet with his belt. What do you think of that?

DENA. Where's he now when I need him.

(**THE FATHER** *hits her with the book, again.*)

THE FATHER. I hear you want to go to college. You want to be different from your old man.

DENA. Yeah, maybe I want to be something better.

THE FATHER. Like what? What are you going to study to make yourself better than your old man?

DENA. I was afraid you were going to ask that.

MYRON. *(proudly)* She's going to be a paleontologist!

THE FATHER. You mean I no longer have to wear disguises to work? Here, I ain't gonna wait. I want you to have my pocket watch now. Let me open it up. By the way, do you see what time it is?

(**DENA** *looks closely at the watch.*)

Uhhhh...

(**THE FATHER** *slams the watch shut on* **DENA**'s *nose.*)

THE FATHER. It's time for you to get outta my house! I don't want to see you come home no more. Stay with your school teacher friend.

DENA. Thanks, I will!

(**THE FATHER** *storms out of the house.* **MYRON** *collapses on the couch and strikes the seat cushions.*)

MYRON. But you can't sleep here. Not here!

DENA. Ok, I'll take the bedroom and you take the couch.

(*Even though* **MYRON** *is fully dressed he reflexively takes a towel and covers his upper torso.*)

MYRON. But…but, you're a girl!

DENA. Thanks for the bulletin.

MYRON. Look, let's go back to three days ago. Here's my wallet with the twenty dollars still in it. Take anything else you want in my apartment. Just rob me and go away.

DENA. We don't want to rob you professor.

MYRON. Sure you do. Here, let me help you carry my stereo to your car.

(**KNUCKLES** *picks up the stereo.*)

KNUCKLES. Check!

(**DENA** *takes the stereo from* **KNUCKLES.** *and puts it back down.*)

DENA. We don't want your stereo. We want to enroll in your class.

MYRON. Anything but that! Look, silver candlesticks. Do you have any idea how much these are worth? You can even hit me on the head with one. Go ahead, right in the back of the head.

(**KNUCKLES** *picks up a candlestick.*)

KNUCKLES. Well ok.

(**DENA** *takes the candlestick from* **KNUCKLES** *and puts* *it back down.)*

DENA. You got to calm down, Professor. Com'on Knuckles, let's put him under the shower and snap him out of this.

(**DENA** *and* **KNUCKLES** *grab a struggling* **MYRON** *by the arms and force him towards the bathroom.)*

MYRON. I won't go! I won't go! Not unless you promise to fill up the bathtub and drown me!

DENA. We ain't gonna drown you. We're your friends.

MYRON. I don't want any friends, I want my apartment!

DENA. Com'on, Professor. We'll splash a little cold water on you and you'll feel like a new man.

(They carry **MYRON** *offstage.)*

DENA *(O.S.)* Ok, Knuckles, turn on the faucet.

KNUCKLES *(O.S.)* Nothing. Bone dry.

DENA *(O.S.)* Son-of-a-Gun. It's dry alright.

(The three of them re-enter the living room.)

MYRON. *(loudly)* The water's been turned off!

(A loud thumping emanates from above.)

MAN'S VOICE. *(O.S.)* And that's not the only thing that's going to get turned off unless you come up with your rent! The lights are next, ya bum ya!

MYRON. Perfect day. Just perfect. I can't even end it all by drowning myself. I can't even end it all.

KNUCKLES. Well…I don't know…Maybe the gas is still on.

(**DENA** *hits* **KNUCKLES** *and motions him to keep quiet. He begins to gather his papers.)*

DENA. Well that's it I guess. If I can't stay here, I'll have to get a job. Which means I can't go to school. Which means you'll lose your job. Which means I'll be saving you a place in the unemployment line.

(Walks up to **MYRON.***)*

DENA. *(cont'd)* And just think…I thought you was gonna be like a father to me. Com'on Knuckles, let's go. Kids like us just aren't meant to get a break.

MYRON. Wait!

DENA. Yes.

MYRON. *(pause)* No! No! Never!

(The lights in the apartment go out. A solitary beam of moonlight coming in the window illuminates **MYRON**, *whose expression turns into profound resignation.)*

MYRON. Never would I think of letting you leave.

DENA. Really! That's great! Knuckles, explain to the super that the professor will be gettin' a check shortly. Have him turn the water and lights back on now.

KNUCKLES. Right.

DENA. Oh, you might also tell him not to bother us no more. Tell him we're students who have difficulty concentrating on our studies.

*(***DENA*** walks over by the window and is illuminated by the beam of moonlight.)*

Tell him we can't always remember if paleontology is about digging up things that are buried…or about burying things that we don't dig.

(Blackout.)

End of Scene 3, Act I

Scene 4

(*AT RISE:* **MYRON** *is sifting through a pile of fossil fragments at his desk. He is painstakingly piecing them together creating a skeletal model.* **KNUCKLES** *is sitting down on the floor in front of the TV eating take-out chicken, and flicking the bones in the same pile that* **MYRON** *is removing them from and examining with a magnifying glass.* **MYRON** *becomes increasingly excited and appears to act like a man on the eve of a great discovery.*)

MYRON. Incredible! Absolutely incredible! It had wings! A species of sub-humanoid actually capable of flight! It flew! It flew!

(**MYRON** *leaps from desk to chair to couch flapping his arms.*)

It flew, I tell you! Why this discovery ranks me with likes of Darwin, Pasteur, Einstein!

(**KNUCKLES** *gets up, hungrily chomping on a chicken-wing, barely able to talk with all the food in his mouth.*)

KNUCKLES. That's great, Professor! You get money for discoveries like that?

MYRON. Are you kidding? I'll be able to write my own ticket! So the landlord is thinking of keeping my deposit, eh?

(*He kicks a hole in the wall.*)

Well now he's got a *real* reason to keep it!

(**KNUCKLES** *views this vandalism with yearning eyes. It is not lost on* **MYRON**.)

Be my guest.

(**KNUCKLES** *kicks an even larger hole in the wall.*)

That should do it, my boy. After all we don't want to displace any termites. They've already got so much invested in this dump.

(**KNUCKLES** *begins picking his teeth.*)

MYRON. *(cont'd)* Knuckles, to you goes the privilege of being the first one to shake the hand of the next Noble Prize winner.

(**MYRON** *and* **KNUCKLES** *shake hands enthusiastically. But the smile slowly dissolves from* **MYRON**'s *face as he stops, feels something in his hand other than* **KNUCKLES** *hand, and pulls out a chicken-bone. He sees the Chicken take-out box on the floor.*)

KNUCKLES. So you think you'll get cash or a check?

MYRON. Chicken??!!

KNUCKLES. Colonel Ming's Oriental Back Porch Fried Chicken Wings. Want some?

(**MYRON** *looks at the damage on the wall.*)

MYRON. I'd rather have some paint and plaster.

KNUCKLES. Ok, but the chicken's fresher.

(**MYRON** *wants to strike him, but relents and pats him on the shoulder.*)

MYRON. It's not your fault. Why only 10,000,000 years ago you probably would have been considered ahead of your time. You might have been worshipped as a God. The most brilliant anthropoid of your era.

KNUCKLES. Gee thanks, Professor. Here, have the fortune cookie.

MYRON. I'm already very aware of what my fortune is, thank you.

KNUCKLES. Aw, go on. Take it. It might make you feel better.

MYRON. Why, is there cyanide in it?

KNUCKLES. They always seem to predict my future.

MYRON. How can you say that! You're a grown...an intelligent...a 20th century...Ok, gimme the cookie.

KNUCKLES. Here you go.

(**MYRON** *opens the cookie and reads the fortune.*)

MYRON. "The road ahead will be bumpy." Humph! See what I mean. It's telling a guy who's already living in a pothole that he's surrounded by a bumpy road. Surprise, surprise!

(There is a knock on the door.)

MYRON. Get that. I don't need any more interruptions.

*(**MYRON** goes back to his desk. **KNUCKLES.** opens the door. A **MAN** wearing a ski-mask is standing on the other side pointing a gun. **KNUCKLES** closes the door.)*

KNUCKLES. It's for you.

MYRON. I'm just not going to get any work done!

*(**MYRON** gets up from his desk, walks over to the door, opens it and sees the **MAN** wearing the ski mask pointing the gun at him.)*

MYRON. That figures.

*(The **MAN** fires the gun.)*

(Blackout.)

End of Scene 4, Act 1

Scene 5

(AT RISE: Moments afterward. **MYRON** *is bent over. The* **MAN** *wearing a ski-mask is standing by the door. After a moment* **MYRON** *straightens up and starts examining his body for a bullet wound he cannot find.)*

MYRON. What the...?!

(The **MAN** *removes his ski-mask revealing it is in fact,* **THE FATHER.***)*

THE FATHER. Is that how you protect my daughter while she's living with you? Just open the door before you find out who's on the other side?

*(***DENA** *enters from the bedroom door.)*

DENA. Jeeze, Dad! What are you doing here?

THE FATHER. Maybe I'm worried about you. Maybe I don't think this bum can take care of you.

MYRON. You nearly gave me a heart attack!

THE FATHER. Aw take it easy, you're fine. Here, have some beer nuts.

*(***THE FATHER** *hands* **MYRON** *a can and he opens it. Several coiled steel snakes pop out.)*

MYRON. Aaaahhhhh!

THE FATHER. That could have just as easily been a bomb. Do you always accept gifts from people you don't know? Do you know what kind of nuts are running around? Is this what you call taking care of my daughter?

DENA. Oh brother!

THE FATHER. Tell me Dena, where do you sleep at night?

DENA. On the couch.

THE FATHER. And where does he make you shower? In the sink? And look at all this junk food. Say Buddy, what's your idea of a balanced meal? Something that doesn't fall off the plate?

DENA. What do you want, anyway?

THE FATHER. Well I thought you might be more happy here if I brought you a few of your things.

MYRON. What things?

(**THE FATHER** *takes a jar out of his pocket.*)

THE FATHER. Her scorpion.

DENA. Stingy!

MYRON. You can't keep a scorpion in here! Especially not one named "Stingy"!

THE FATHER. What's the problem? He eats leftovers and sleeps in the jar. Just pretend you're taking care of another one of my kids.

MYRON. But why is he in a jar labeled "peanuts"?

DENA. Because the jar labeled "caviar" is on my yacht back at the marina.

MYRON. That's not what I mean! How can you keep a dangerous insect inside something that any unsuspecting person could just put his hand inside?

THE FATHER. Will you forget about that and help me bring her trunk in.

MYRON. Trunk?

THE FATHER. Let's go, let's go.

(**THE FATHER** *grabs* **MYRON**, *then stares at* **DENA** *for a moment.*)

THE FATHER. Jeeze Dena, I don't know what it is but you look different.

(**THE FATHER** *and* **MYRON** *exit through the back door as* **KNUCKLES** *approaches* **DENA**. *He stares at her then it hits him.*)

KNUCKLES. A dress! You're wearing a dress! Why are you wearing a dress?

DENA. Because I'm a girl, stupid. Sometimes girls wear dresses.

(**KNUCKLES** *just keeps looking at* **DENA**.)

What's wrong now?

KNUCKLES. Nothing. Just never saw your legs before.

DENA. Well keep staring and you won't have to worry about them anymore because I'm going to poke both your eyes out with my thumbs.

KNUCKLES. Sorry.

DENA. Well?

KNUCKLES. Well what?

DENA. (*Impatiently*) Well what do you think of them?

(**KNUCKLES** *slowly walks around* **DENA.**)

KNUCKLES. Um…uh…let's see. They come in a pair. And uh, they both reach the ground. So I guess they're ok.

DENA. Glad I asked.

KNUCKLES. Now I've got a question for you.

DENA. What?

KNUCKLES. Have you seen the class schedule?

(*HE hands* **DENA** *a piece of paper*)

DENA. Yeah, I already saw it.

KNUCKLES. According to that, the field trip to the museum isn't for two months yet. Two months!

DENA. Don't panic.

KNUCKLES. Don't panic? We gotta wait two months before we can pull off this heist and I have a book report due next week!

DENA. I know, I know. Maybe I made a small mistake in this operation. This job calls for more direct action.

KNUCKLES. Now you're talking! I say when the professor comes in we bash him on the head, knock out a few of his teeth, break his thumbs and then ask him for the key to the museum basement.

DENA. Why don't we just ask him for the key first?

KNUCKLES. Because he might give it to us!

DENA. Well get all those ideas out of your head. We ain't gonna hurt the professor. He took me in when my own father kicked me out.

KNUCKLES. Then how do we get in?

DENA. I guess the only way to get in the museum basement is if we actually discover something of value worth putting in. Time to crack those books again.

KNUCKLES. No, no, no, no! That's not why we're here!

(**TILLY** *enters through the front door.*)

TILLY. What are you doing here? Where's Myron…I mean Professor Amberworth?

DENA. Moo Moo…I mean Myron is downstairs. And why shouldn't I be here. I live here.

TILLY. Nonsense. Myron would never live in the same apartment with a young girl. I know. And I'm practically his fiancée.

DENA. Well, I'm practically the Queen of England, but between my butt and a throne to park it on lies a whole lot of real estate, Sister.

TILLY. How sweet. You've developed a crush on Myron! I remember my own experience with puppy love.

DENA. You mean somebody else thought you was a dog too?

TILLY. I mean, dear child, it's perfectly normal for a youngster of your age to become infatuated with someone older than yourself. I just hoped you might have picked someone who didn't have any…attachments.

DENA. But it's just his attachments I like. He's sorta like a big vacuum cleaner. And I bet he picks up things real easy too.

TILLY. Just careful you don't plug it in.

DENA. How else do I turn it on?

(**MYRON** *walks in.*)

MYRON. Hello, Ladies.

KNUCKLES. (*To* **MYRON**) You got here just in time professor. I think they were getting ready to clean the apartment.

TILLY. Myron, is it true these kids are living here with you?

MYRON. No.

(**TILLY** *looks at* **DENA** *and smiles.*)

MYRON. Just Dena is.

TILLY. Myron how can you! What does her father say?

MYRON. He's bringing over her trunk now.

TILLY. Myron!

MYRON. It's not what you think. It's a long story.

TILLY. I have time.

MYRON. Well…you look pretty wound up all right. Ha, ha, ha. Oh boy.

DENA. Say professor, before you bring her up on the facts of life can I ask you a question? If Knuckles and me found something of interest inside a rock would it have to be put inside the museum basement?

MYRON. Well I suppose…at first. If it's of paleontological interest. But…

KNUCKLES. And the larger a rock is the better the chance of finding something inside?

MYRON. If it's the proper type of formation, yes. I guess it stands to reason, the larger the rock the better but…

DENA. Thanks, Professor.

(**DENA** and **KNUCKLES** *exit.*)

MYRON. See darling. It's strictly business. I'll get her a new place as soon as I can. It's just that her father kicked her out of his house.

TILLY. He seems like a wonderful man.

MYRON. I don't know how I got into all of this.

TILLY. Oh lets forget about them, Myron. Come here. Sit down beside me.

(**TILLY** and **MYRON** *sit on the couch.*)

If we are going to get married soon, don't you think it's time we think about having children. You do want to have children, don't you?

(**DENA** and **KNUCKLES** *enter, rolling a large boulder across the floor into the bedroom.*)

MYRON. No.

(**MYRON** *walks up to the bedroom and yells.*)

I want that rock out of here!

KNUCKLES *(O.S.)* But it could be important.

MYRON. Why? Did it fall out of your head?

DENA *(O.S.)* We'll get it out in a minute.

MYRON. Do you know how heavy that is? We're on the second floor!

(There is a loud sound of something crashing through the floor and landing below. A car's horn is heard sounding in the distance. **KNUCKLES** *and* **DENA** *walk sheepishly into the room.)*

KNUCKLES. Ok. It's out.

DENA. I think, however, your theory about the bigger the rock the better could use a little fine tuning.

KNUCKLES. Along with your car.

DENA. But the horn sounds fine. Good pitch. Why don't me and Knuckles go downstairs and see what we can do to salvage it.

*(***KNUCKLES*** and ***DENA*** exit quickly.)*

MYRON. Oh yeah! Oh yeah! I want to have kids. And I want to jump in front of a moving train wearing only my underwear!

TILLY. Myron not all kids are like...

MYRON. How do you know not all kids are like them? How do you know these two aren't the shiniest models off the showroom floor? And you can't trade them in after you get them! No. You gotta keep them for at least 18 years. Doesn't matter how much smoke they belch or how much fuel they consume, you gotta keep them. Well not me, Sister!

TILLY. Myron. What are you saying?

MYRON. We aren't going to have any kids!

TILLY. You're excited.

MYRON. I'm insane!

TILLY. I insist on having children!

MYRON. Fine. You can insist on having a root canal, too! But don't expect me to be in the same room with you when you have either.

TILLY. I never want to see you again. Moo Moo!

(**TILLY** *storms out of the room.*)

MYRON. Moo Moo? Darling! No! Wait!

(**KNUCKLES** *enters with a broken steering wheel pretending he's driving, making varoom, varoom noises. He stops when he sees* **MYRON** *isn't smiling.*)

KNUCKLES. I know it don't look like much now, professor. But imagine it surrounded by a new front and rear end as your driving along the expressway.

(**MYRON** *takes the steering wheel from* **KNUCKLES**.)

MYRON. Gee. I already feel the wind whipping through my hair.

KNUCKLES. That's a positive attitude.

MYRON. I'm a positive kind of guy now. I'm positive how I'm about to add to the paleontology record of the future. Ha ha. Ha ha ha!

KNUCKLES. Ha ha. Ha ha ha! How you gonna do that?

(**MYRON** *laughs maniacally, and* **KNUCKLES** *joins in good naturedly.* **MYRON** *quickly delivers a series of punches into* **KNUCKLES** *stomach, karate chops to the neck and wraps his arms around him in a crushing bear hug and squeezes with all his might, all to no effect.*)

MYRON. Hmmm…I don't suppose if I threw a nice shinny ball into the center of some bubbling tar pits and asked you to get it for me, you would?

KNUCKLES. (*Thinking*) Naahhhh…I don't think so, Professor.

MYRON. Well fine for you! I lost Tilly. I don't have my apartment to myself anymore. You won't play in the tar pits. What's the point of it all! From now on, its just me for me, so look out world. There's nothing more dangerous than a rebellious paleontologist with some real bones to pick.

(*Blackout.*)

End of Scene 5, Act I

Scene 6

*(**SETTING**: Same small bachelor apartment.)*

*(**AT RISE**: Morning. Seated at the desk is **DENA**. She is on the telephone. She is wearing a hair ribbon in the shape of a butterfly.)*

DENA. What do you mean you haven't seen him? He's a teacher there! Well ok. But call me if he comes in.

*(**DENA** puts down the telephone, and puts on a pair of reading glasses and starts going over some papers. **KNUCKLES** walks in the door, sees her, quietly picks up a magazine, rolls it up, sneaks up behind her and smacks the ribbon in the shape of a butterfly off her head and stomps on it several times.)*

DENA. Ouch!!! Are you crazy? What are you doing?

KNUCKLES. There was a giant butterfly on your head. I think it was getting ready to lay eggs.

DENA. That ain't a butterfly you idiot! It's a hair ribbon!

KNUCKLES. It is a ribbon. You were wearing a hair ribbon! Why are you wearing a hair ribbon?

DENA. To keep the hair out of my eyes. That way I can see better when I want to knock the dandruff off of your head!

(She hits him on the head several times with the magazine.)

KNUCKLES. I got dandruff?

DENA. Focus, Knuckles. Did you find the professor?

KNUCKLES. Nah! Nobody's seen him.

DENA. Well get back out there and find him!

*(**KNUCKLES** exits through the front door as **MYRON** enters through the rear door. **MYRON** moves and acts like a troubled teenager. He is wearing a swim suit with a towel draped casually over him shoulders.)*

DENA. Professor, where have you been? What are you wearing?

MYRON. These are my new threads, square girl.

DENA. Did you finish grading yesterday's papers?

MYRON. Maybe I don't feel like it.

DENA. Hey, how do you think this world would be if we only did things we felt like doing?

MYRON. *(muttering)* I wish you felt like taking a running jump into an empty pool.

DENA. What was that?

MYRON. Nothing, nothing, I didn't say nothing. Now I gotta get to the beach. Surf's up chicky-pooh.

DENA. Look, take a seat, Professor.

*(**DENA** and **MYRON** sit on the couch. **MYRON** softly starts kicking the table leg.)*

DENA. And quit kicking the furniture! Now I know you've had a fight with Miss Plumms. It will work itself out. But you can't go on like this. I can't keep covering for you and they're gonna fire you if you don't show up at school soon. What's Tilly going to say if you lose your job?

*(**MYRON** walks over to a pair of pictures of Tilly and himself hanging on the wall side by side.)*

MYRON. Tilly. She did say she'd always be there for me.

(The vibration of the passing train makes Tilly's picture fall to the ground.)

MYRON. A lot she cares! I wish I was never born!

*(**MYRON** runs out.)*

DENA. That does it. Tonight, I'm calling his parents. Maybe a year teaching in Military School might straighten him out.

*(**DENA** picks up the fallen picture of Tilly to hang it back up but then changes her mind.)*

Come to think of it, it looks better on the floor.

*(**KNUCKLES** walks in the front door.)*

KNUCKLES. Say was that the Professor running down the stairs?

DENA. Yeah, he's just become a rebel. And he's off to the beach. Too bad the nearest beach is over 1,000 miles away. Poor guy. There's more to being a troubled delinquent than a bad attitude. There's geography, too.

KNUCKLES. I know. You been trying to teach me that for years.

DENA. And you been doing good. That's why when we go out on jobs you're the driver.

KNUCKLES. I thought it was because your feet couldn't reach the pedals.

DENA. You know Knuckles, it ain't like you're gonna get a whole lot of compliments in your lifetime. Take the ones I give you.

KNUCKLES. Sorry.

DENA. It's this Tilly thing. It's got him bent all out of shape. Not that he didn't have the backbone of a pretzel to begin with. But if he gets fired then we're really in a jam.

(**DENA** *writes a quick note and hands it to* **KNUCKLES**.)

Run this note over to Tilly.

(**KNUCKLES** *exits. After a moment* **LILAH** *walks through the apartment's open door. She has her portable tape recorder hanging from her shoulder.* **DENA** *walks in from the bedroom.*)

LILAH. Say little girl, are your parents home?

DENA. *(looks around)* Well if they are, Granny, they sure don't take up much space now do they?

LILAH. That's cute, kid. Here's a buck. Why don't you buy something adorable and then see if you can imitate it.

DENA. Sure. And if you get bored while I'm gone you can fix your face in the mirror. Or do jobs that big, usually require a permit from the city first?

LILAH. Maybe. I'll call and find out. Does this place have a phone or is your mouth big enough to cover long distance?

DENA. Phone's on the counter. Mirror's in the bathroom. Oh, and in case you get confused, the mirror is the thing that will look just like you, only it will be the one with the personality.

LILAH. Thanks for the tip. Kids really are our country's greatest natural resource. I guess that's why I have this tremendous urge to export them.

(**MYRON** *walks in.*)

DENA. Great, Professor, you're back.

MYRON. Just for more bus fair. I didn't know it was over a thousand miles to the beach.

(**MYRON** *sees* **LILAH.**)

MYRON. Oh excuse, me. Are you looking for someone?

LILAH. I'm Lilah Davenport. Herald Register. I'm here to interview Myron Amberworth.

MYRON. That used to be me. I'm known as Clambake Cubunga now. And I don't know anything about an interview…Baby.

LILAH. No objection I hope. I'm doing an article on recent discoveries in Paleontology.

MYRON. That's too bad. Because I'm kinda getting out the Paleontology thing. It's just chicks and good times now.

LILAH. That's too bad. I always thought science was kinda sexy myself.

MYRON. Really?

LILAH. Sure. I've read quite a few articles by you and your colleague, Dr. Gibbons.

MYRON. Well…yes. Say, you really do like paleontology.

(**LILAH** *draws very close to him, and places her hand on his leg.*)

LILAH. What's not to like? Uncovering magnificent objects…Long kept hidden from prying eyes…Waiting to be seen and handled for the first time…Polished, rubbed and mounted for public display. Wouldn't anybody find that exciting?

MYRON. *(lump in throat)* Well...that does seem to be putting a different angle on it.

DENA. But Professor, didn't you teach us that just because something's hard to find that doesn't make it valuable. That a squirrel that digs up a nut is still just a squirrel...

*(Looks at **LILAH**.)*

...with a nut.

*(Looks at **MYRON**.)*

MYRON. I said that?

DENA. Maybe. Anyway, while you're occupied I'll do some light inventory in the museum.

MYRON. You will not! I'll take care of it. Look Dena, I'm a little busy right now. Don't you have something to do outside?

*(**LILAH** throws **DENA** some keys.)*

LILAH. Yeah, kid, you can use my car. If you have trouble reaching the pedals don't let it worry you. I've got accident insurance.

DENA. If that's true how come you haven't collected on your face yet?

LILAH. Because I'm asking the doctors to work on my butt first. I'd ask you to be the model for it but I don't want one with a mouth that talks.

DENA. I'm sorry. I've been very rude. I apologize. Here, have a peanut.

*(**DENA** presents **LILAH** with the jar containing Stingy, the scorpion, and **MYRON** yanks it away from her.)*

MYRON. Just go!

*(**DENA** exits.)*

LILAH. Sorry. Guess we got off on the wrong foot. Your daughter?

MYRON. No. My student.

LILAH. You just live together?

(She picks up a bra off the sofa.)

MYRON. Well, yeah…

LILAH. Uh huh. I'm actually here to find out about Dr. Givvons latest discoveries.

MYRON. Well he's not ready to reveal anything until the release of his book, *Monkey Dearest: A Personal View of Evolution.* Unfortunately, it ended up being a little too personal for the publisher. I told Dr. Gibbons three years alone in a jungle was a long time.

LILAH. Leaves me without a story. At least one I'd want to print.

MYRON. Sorry. Guess you need to find another story.

*(**LILAH** picks up **DENA**'s bra again and speaks into her tape recorder.)*

LILAH. Today's professor: Wake up, America. How many of these craven Casanovas and depraved Don Juan's are living with young under age girls…

*(**MYRON** turns off the tape recorder.)*

MYRON. What would you like to know?

LILAH. Since Professor Gibbons isn't here I think I'd like to make you the focus of a first hand article about paleontology.

MYRON. Really!

*(**LILAH** places her hand on **MYRON** as **TILLY** walks in carrying in a package.)*

TILLY. Myron, I'm sorry about the other…Darling, who is this?

MYRON. Tilly! You're back! This is Miss Davenport. She writes for a magazine. She wants to do an article about me first hand!

*(**TILLY** removes **LILAH**'s hand from **MYRON**.)*

TILLY. I'm surprised she has one to spare. I'm Tilly, Myron's fiancé. So you want to write an article about my Myron? For your magazine?

LILAH. Yes, I have a feeling he's going to be the biggest thing I'm ever going to put between the covers.

TILLY. Well as you see Myron does have a fascination with old relics, but only for their historic curiosity.

LILAH. I guess that's because newer things today fall apart so easily because they're so cheap to begin with.

MYRON. That's true, I just bought this pencil sharpener that...

TILLY. Shut up, Myron. I mean, couldn't you do this interview over the phone? After all, you are a very busy man.

MYRON. Oh, I'm not that busy. Say what did you bring over?

TILLY. That package you wanted me to pick up at the post office.

(MYRON excitedly takes the package and reads the attached letter.)

MYRON. Oh good. I've been waiting for this to come in.

TILLY. I paid the postage due myself.

MYRON. Fine, Dear...Postman say if any other package was coming?

(MYRON ignores TILLY as he continues reading the contents of the letter. TILLY becomes increasingly annoyed.)

TILLY. Well, he did mention he thought I was a pretty well put together package. And I said thank you but I was a package only to be opened by my loving boyfriend, Myron. And he said he appreciated that but would I object if he tried to steam open a flap. I said sorry but I was already addressed to my boyfriend and that was that. But then he asked if he could at least lick the stamps. And I said certainly not because I was already stuck on Myron. Then he said he didn't think your letter opener was as big as his letter opener. And I politely said maybe not, but he doesn't need one because he doesn't get a lot of mail. But Myron, I resisted all his advances. Aren't I peach!

LILAH. Yeah, you should be hanging from a tree alright.

MYRON. I'm sorry Tilly I wasn't listening. Did you say I owe you postage?

LILAH. Oh never mind!

(**TILLY** *storms out the door.*)

LILAH. Well that made me thirsty. Say, do you drink?

(**LILAH** *leans over* **MYRON** *who puts down the package.*)

MYRON. Well um…a little.

LILAH. I've been known to moisten my lips too.

(**MYRON** *prepares a drink which she downs bottoms up.*)

MYRON. I don't know how much I can tell you about Dr. Gibbons that you probably don't already know. I'm his assistant, it's true. But he's in Africa, or was supposed to be and we haven't communicated much lately.

LILAH. You mix a mean drink, Professor, but I'd still swear that's a package from Dr. Gibbons you're holding.

MYRON. Oh that one. I get them every once in a while from overseas. Just miscellaneous bone fragments, I'm sure. This letter doesn't really say what's inside.

LILAH. Aren't you going to open it?

MYRON. Why bother? I don't get the important specimens. I bet I can describe exactly what it is without looking. I bet I can tell you almost word for word what the accompanying note inside says. I know the drill.

LILAH. I'll wager you a dinner you can't.

MYRON. Ha! You're on.

(*He hands her the box and turns around, covering his eyes. She begins opening the box.*)

MYRON. Let's see. Inside you'll find an ugly little brown rock made out of sandstone. Have I put my finger on it?

(*She pulls out a diamond the size of a doorknob.*)

LILAH. Let's just say I do see it on a finger.

MYRON. Ha! You owe me dinner. So whatdaya have?

LILAH. Oh, about 150 carats.

MYRON. Darn. A vegetarian.

(He takes his hand off his eyes and starts to turn around. **LILAH** *stops him.)*

LILAH. Not so fast! You forgot to tell me what the note says.

MYRON. Don't know when to give up, do you?

LILAH. I guess you're just too smart. But humor me, ok.

(She takes the diamond and the enclosed note and puts it in her purse. She takes a paperweight made out of a rock off the desk and places it in the box)

MYRON. Let's see. Something to the effect of, "Dear Myron: Enclosed please find more samples of the sedimentary deposit I recently unearthed from the excavation site."

*(***LILAH*** exits.)*

And of course, there will be the usual ending. Like, uh, "Please be very careful with the contents and do not lose them." As though I'm some kind of an idiot.

(Blackout.)

End of Scene 6, Act I

Scene 7

(AT RISE: **MYRON** *is working at his desk. A ladder is propped up against the open window from outside. A* **FIREMAN** *wearing an oxygen mask climbs up and yells.)*

FIREMAN. Gas leak! Evacuate the building.

*(***MYRON** *rushes up to the window.)*

MYRON. Gas leak? Should I come down the ladder?

FIREMAN. Sure. You forget anything?

MYRON. No.

FIREMAN. Oh really? What about my daughter?

(The **FIREMAN** *tears off his mask revealing it is* **THE FATHER***, and hits* **MYRON** *on top of the head with his fire helmet.* **MYRON** *falls over backwards.)*

MYRON. Yeeeooow! You again!

THE FATHER. Lucky it is just me! So in a real emergency you think about yourself and leave my daughter to make it out on her own, huh?

MYRON. *(steaming)* Your daughter is at the library!

THE FATHER. Well pardon me all to hell! You see, it's not as easy as you think being a father.

MYRON. Look you, if don't like the job I'm doing, why don't you take her home with you. You started this whole thing!

THE FATHER. Who me? Compete with you? Maybe I could if I weren't so busy all the time. Right now I gotta return this fire truck.

*(***THE FATHER** *exits and* **LILAH** *enters.)*

LILAH. I came back, Myron. Crazy huh? I could spend the rest of my life in prison. But I don't care. I've fallen for you hard, Myron. Maybe because I knew I could never outwit you and I'm crazy about guys who have the smarts.

MYRON. So where's the eats?

LILAH. Huh? You mean you still don't know?

MYRON. Well, I know I'm hungry. There's a little Italian restaurant...

LILAH. Right. Well, bye. Gotta go.

(He grabs her.)

MYRON. Just a second. What's going on here anyway? I thought we had a date?

*(The phone rings and **MYRON** answers it.)*

MYRON. What's that operator? Africa? Yes. Put him through. Hello professor. What are you doing in Africa? I thought you were in Istanbul. Got too hot in Istanbul? Aren't you wearing your pith helmet? Yes, Doctor, I'll shut up. Yes, I got the package. Oh yes, very exciting.

*(**MYRON** stifles a giggle and mockingly gestures "Whoopee" with his hand. **LILAH** forces a laugh.)*

MYRON. No, it's *not* in a safety deposit box. Well for the moment, it's just sitting on top of my desk.

*(**MYRON** quickly moves the phone away from his ear and massages his ear canal with his little finger.)*

MYRON. Please, Doctor, you don't have to yell. What's the matter? But I *want* to keep it on my desk. Because I'm using it as a paperweight. Hello? Doctor? Oh Doctor? Hmm...we've been disconnected.

LILAH. Well don't worry about it. Transatlantic line you know.

MYRON. That must be it. Because I could have sworn I heard a lot of gurgling.

LILAH. Look, Myron, I like you. You may not believe that later, but it's true.

MYRON. What are you talking about?

LILAH. I just want you to promise you'll give me a chance later to explain it to you. You've got to promise me that. Don't despise me, Myron. Don't hate me. Promise you won't hate me.

(**LILAH** *gives* **MYRON** *the most passionate kiss he's ever known.*)

MYRON. Could you repeat that last part.

(**LILAH** *gives* **MYRON** *another passionate kiss*)

MYRON. That's what I thought you said.

(**LILAH** *gets up and prepares to leave.*)

LILAH. You'll hear things about me, Myron. Ugly things. Awful things. But in your heart I know you'll remember me as the woman who would have done anything for you. You only had to ask.

MYRON. Does that include dinner?

LILAH. No.

(**LILAH** *exits through back door.*)

MYRON. Wait!

(**MYRON** *exits.* **TILLY** *enters through front door and looks around. Moments later* **DENA** *and* **KNUCKLES** *enter.*)

TILLY. Where's Myron? If that lady thinks she's going to take him away from me she's got another thing coming!

KNUCKLES. Good, good.

(**TILLY** *takes a picture of* **MYRON** *out of her purse and looks at it adoringly.* **DENA** *looks at it too, and seems to soften and starts to smile.*)

DENA. Wow…So that's what he looks like when he's not yelling.

(*There is a knock on the door*)

OFFSTAGE VOICE. Telegram.

(**DENA** *opens up the door and takes the telegram. She tries to close the door but the* **BOY** *from Western-Union is blocking it with his foot.*)

DENA. Knuckles. The kid wants a tip. Take care of it.

KNUCKLES. Knuckles do this, Knuckles do that. What am I, a servant? Just this guy who doesn't know anything but senseless violence. Well I got a brain too, gal!

(**KNUCKLES** *walks up to the door, stomps on the foot of the* **BOY** *from Western Union, who yells.* **KNUCKLES** *then shuts the door.*)

KNUCKLES. *(cont'd)* And I'm through unless you start treating me like it!

DENA. You're right, Knuckles. Sorry.

KNUCKLES. Well…ok then.

DENA. Hey what do you know. A telegram for the professor from Africa.

KNUCKLES. Ah ha! Africa. One of the seven consonants!

DENA. Yeah…thanks. Hey, I wonder if we should open it up.

(**TILLY** *grabs the telegram from* **DENA.**)

TILLY. Don't you dare!

DENA. It's from Dr. Gibbons.

TILLY. *(with contempt)* Oh, him! Maybe we should open it. I mean it could be urgent. Myron is a very important man whom the doctor relies on for his keen judgement.

(*She opens the telegram and reads:*)

"Myron you ninny! STOP If I could I'd crush your feeble head like a crenshaw melon and happily accept the consequences STOP The object you are using as a paperweight is significantly more valuable than you think STOP Guard it with your life until I return STOP Reply immediately STOP END TRANSMISSION"

(**TILLY**, **DENA** *and* **KNUCKLES** *walk over to the desk.* **TILLY** *picks up the paperweight.*)

TILLY. Guard this with your life?

DENA. It says, "Chicago World's Fair" on the bottom.

(**KNUCKLES** *takes the paperweight from* **DENA.**)

KNUCKLES. Of course!

DENA. What?

KNUCKLES. *Continents.* I meant to say Africa is one of the seven *continents.*

DENA. Great. Shoot up a flare know when you get within visual sight of us. Now why is this thing so valuable?

TILLY. And why did Myron keep it a secret from me?

DENA. He kept it a secret from all of us.

TILLY. Including the lady reporter? I wonder. I think…I think it's time for a general accounting with Myron.

(**TILLY** *exits.*)

DENA. Would the professor keep a secret from me too? I mean I can understand why he'd want to hold out on his dippy girlfriend.

(**KNUCKLES** *sniffs the air.*)

KNUCKLES. What's that smell?

(**DENA** *quickly moves away from him, but* **KNUCKLES** *follows her.*)

DENA. I don't smell nothing'.

KNUCKLES. It's…it's you! You're wearing perfume!

DENA. Some saleslady in a store spritzed me with the stuff when I wasn't looking. That's all.

KNUCKLES. I'll open the windows.

DENA. It, uh…won't help. I…I bought a bottle of the stuff. Funny, huh?

(*An unsmiling* **KNUCKLES** *just stares at her.*)

DENA. Look, Knuckles, they don't give out a door prize for smelling like yesterdays laundry.

KNUCKLES. Some things you do just because you know it's right!

DENA. Well…get used to it.

KNUCKLES. Boy, you think I'm dumb. But I can see something you can't see. Or don't wanna.

DENA. What are you talking about?

KNUCKLES. We ain't gonna rob the professor. Because you're in love with him!

(**KNUCKLES** *exits.*)

DENA. Hey what?! You crazy?! Come back here! Me?! In love with old Four-eyes?! Eyes that are soft blue azure... Eyes the color of a languid lake in spring just after the first rains have fallen. Eyes like gentle reflecting pools, calm but deep. Me? In love? Ridiculous!

(**DENA** *exits into bedroom,* **MYRON** *enters back door panting.*)

MYRON. Something very odd is going on here. She must be halfway to Timbuktu by now.

(**LILAH** *enters front door, looking refreshed and beautiful in a new dress.*)

LILAH. Myron. Thank God you're still here!

MYRON. Where have you been?

LILAH. Myron you magnificent beast. I suddenly realized you were acting for my benefit. Playing dumb for me you crazy lug. You know what I did but you're going to take responsibility for it because...because you really do care. And you were brilliant enough to figure it out. And damn you, Myron, I can't resist a guy with brains.

MYRON. Thank you. You see I realized that everything was going fine until I figured out you don't like Italian food. Fortunately, I remembered this Chinese restaurant...

LILAH. I think I'm double parked. Bye.

(**LILAH** *exits through front door.*)

MYRON. Come back here!

(**MYRON** *exits, and* **DENA** *enters from bedroom. She is carrying a compact, and when she is sure there is no one else around she walks up to the mirror and starts applying lipstick to herself*).

DENA. Could it be? Me...and the professor?

(*The door opens and* **THE FATHER** *enters. He watches his daughter with concern. He spins her around, and becomes angry.*)

THE FATHER. My God! Your lips. So the bum went and hit my baby!

DENA. It ain't blood pop.

THE FATHER. But your lips, they're red.

DENA. I been eating persimmons, ok!

THE FATHER. That ain't persimmons. You look…you look just like your dear mother when we first met over 18 years ago. Pomegranate! You been eating pomegranate!

DENA. Yeah, you caught me. Pomegranate. Say, why aren't you at work?

THE FATHER. I give up my job with the construction company. If my daughter likes living with a pale gynecologist so much, then I can't do no better than become one myself.

DENA. I'm not studying to become a pale gynecologist! It's paleontologist!

THE FATHER. Oh. Well now what do I do with this book I already bought?

(**THE FATHER** *removes a book from underneath his shirt and shows it to* **DENA**, *who opens it up and quickly closes it again.*)

DENA. Better let me have it. If Ma catches you with it she'll brain you.

(**DENA** *puts the book down on the couch.*)

What's gotten into you pop? You can't quit your job. You just made foreman of the crew. You were in the middle of building a bridge.

(**THE FATHER** *puts his arm around* **DENA**. *and speaks gently.*)

THE FATHER. I'm building another bridge now. One between my daughter and me.

DENA. Aw, Pop…

(**THE FATHER** *slaps* **DENA** *on the ears.*)

THE FATHER. Stand up straight when I'm talking to you!

DENA. Hey, why all the time you gotta be hitting me?

THE FATHER. You're right, darling. I'm sorry. That's no way for Paleontologists to behave. By the way, do you think I could stay with you and the professor for awhile. Your mother kicked me out of the house when I told her of my career change.

DENA. Well... That's gonna be kinda tough now Dad. I mean, the way things are now between the professor and me.

THE FATHER. (*through clenched teeth*) What do you mean, the way things are now between you and the professor?

DENA. Well, I...I think, we're gonna get married.

THE FATHER. He asked you to marry him?

DENA. Not in so many words. The professor is a busy man.

THE FATHER. Well...maybe I can help him slow down a little.

DENA. You ain't mad?

THE FATHER. Not at all. In fact, I'm gonna buy a gift for him right now.

DENA. Remember, it don't have to be big.

THE FATHER. Big? Let's just say it's something I'll be carrying over here inside a barrel!

(**THE FATHER** *exits.*)

DENA. Really? Wow! I can't believe it. This is great!

(*She turns on the radio. Music plays over the station, and* **DENA** *dances to it, eventually dancing her way into the bedroom. The music suddenly stops. An announcer comes on the station*)

ANNOUNCER. Flash! Police are looking for a Dr. Ebon Gibbons, an apparently deranged professor of Paleontology, who escaped from customs moments ago while trying to enter the U.S. Before escaping, Dr. Gibbons leaped on the counter brandishing a pistol he had taken from a customs official. Sources at the scene quoted Dr. Gibbons as screaming something about dying penniless but that he didn't care as long as he could take that boob with him. Police advise anyone who may in fact be the boob in question to please lock his or her doors. Thank you. We now return you to your listening pleasure.

(Blackout.)

End of Scene 7, Act I

Scene 8

*(**AT RISE:** Evening. Dark empty room. **MYRON** enters through the front door, panting, sweating and rumpled. He turns on the light. **LILAH** is there, sitting in a chair, waiting for Him. She looks cool, relaxed and beautiful in a different dress.)*

MYRON. You're here!?

LILAH. Where should I be, Myron? Where can I escape from the Hell that's been my life ever since I met you? What corner of the Earth can hide my shattered life? A life that's tasted love, real love for the first time, and is now choking my spirit little by little.

MYRON. Well I think…

LILAH. Ever met a Hollywood producer with more arms than an octopus? Or an Advertising Executive with more hands than a riverboat gambler? I've been pawed more often than the ground around a dog track. And I've been mishandled more times than airport luggage on an international flight. All right, Myron, I did it. I did it. And why shouldn't I have. What do I owe the world. I've been used so now it's my turn. Little Lilah Davenport. The girl most likely to take it on the chin. But when I opened that package it seemed so clear to me. I could cool down a lot of martinis with that chunk of ice, baby. I thought I had it all figured out. But I was wrong. Just like the captain of the Titanic was wrong over 50 years ago. He forgot like I forgot that you can't see 9/10 of the danger. It lurks just beneath the surface, and when I remembered your trusting eyes your kind hands I knew I had been wrong. I had used all the dirt that had been done to me not to get back at the world. No. But to justify my own greed. My own insatiable lust for money. And now I can't go through with it Myron, I can't go through with it!

MYRON. Lilah, I want you to tell me the truth. We're not talking about dinner anymore are we?

LILAH. Still playing the confused little boy. Oh, Myron, hold me.

(LILAH *jumps off the chair and rushes to* MYRON *who holds her in his arms.*)

LILAH. I had a dream, Myron. I was driving down a dirt road late at night. I kept going because I was afraid the next stop might be my last. I was afraid the next stop would mean my murder.

(*The lights begin to fade very slowly, and the bedroom door begins to open slightly casting a beam of light across the floor that neither of them sees.*)

MYRON. Get a hold of yourself, Lilah. It was just a dream. If I believed every dream I had, I would have pitched the 9th inning of the last game of the world series in leotards and a tutu.

(*The lights continue to fade slowly. The bedroom door continues to open wider*)

LILAH. I feel odd, Myron. Just the way I felt once before, when a doctor had to put me under. His hands were cold. Like death. Hold me, Myron. I need a real man to hold me.

MYRON. Of course, the leotards and tutu part used to bother me. But my analyst said not to worry about it because it just meant that I was artistic. Odd though, that he giggled when he said it. Hmmm... .

(*The lights fade further. A gloved hand holding a gun aimed at* MYRON *and* LILAH *is slowly revealed coming from behind the open door.*)

LILAH. The hairs on my arms are standing on end, Myron. My teeth are on edge. What is it I'm sensing? Like something inside me knows that death is near. But From where? From who? Myron, talk to me. Say the things I need to hear.

MYRON. I mean it's not like I played with dolls or anything when I was a kid. G.I. Joe doesn't count, does he? No, of course not. But what about that weekend he spent with Ken?

(Lights fade to black. Several shots ring out. A body is heard falling to the floor. A baby in the next apartment begins to cry. General commotion. A siren is heard in the distance.)

End of Act I

ACT II

Scene 1

(SETTING: Bare. Black.)

(AT RISE: Spotlight on **LILAH DAVENPORT**. *Her pace is slow and measured. She walks up to the audience and stops.)*

LILAH. They counted over half-a-dozen bullet holes in me and my Pucci Designer Original. Ironic when I remember I bought the dress specifically because it had a zipper because I didn't even like button holes.

*(***LILAH** *crosses from one end of the stage to the other.)*

Funny. There weren't any cops around when I came to the end. But within minutes of my hitting the carpet I was surrounded by more flatfoots than a cheap podiatrist after a walk-a-thon. It didn't take the blue-review more than an hour to escort me downtown. I made it alright. I was the grand marshall in my own private motorcade. Only there were no cheering crowds lining the streets, and instead of the key to the city all I got was a cold slab made out of marble – Formaldehyde by the gallon, but nobody to drink it with me. I was gone alright. But Myron was still alive. And he would only continue to stay alive if he were smart enough to realize I was still there by his side.

(Blackout.)

End of Scene 1, Act II

Scene 2

(SETTING: MYRON's apartment.)

(AT RISE: It is late at night and MYRON and TILLY are sitting on the couch holding each other. There is a very sexy and shapely chalk outline on the floor in front of them, which they are staring at.)

TILLY. Myron, can't we put some newspapers over it or something.

MYRON. I don't know. It might be tampering with evidence.

TILLY. But it's just her chalk outline. And if you ask me the policeman who drew it was being just a little too flattering to her.

MYRON. Oh...I don't know.

TILLY. Myron, will you please stop that. You're ogling a chalk outline.

MYRON. I am not!

TILLY. Humph! I wonder if you would show that much interest in my own chalk outline.

MYRON. Darling, I don't know any woman whose chalk outline I'd rather view than yours. Let's just talk about something else.

TILLY. I just wish the police would finish.

MYRON. The police won't be back tonight. I still can't believe she's gone. Just like that. Her tape recorder is all that's left.

TILLY. I guess you...cared about her.

MYRON. I won't lie to you. Yes, I did care. But not in the way you think. You see, for some strange reason she looked up to me. She was a kid really. She needed the strength, conviction and wisdom of an older man.

(MYRON absentmindedly turns on the tape recorder and LILAH's voice is heard.)

LILAH. *(Recorded Voice)* "It's hard to believe anyone as weak, dotty and indecisive as Myron Amberworth can rise to the level of University professor."

(**MYRON** *quickly turns off the recorder.*)

MYRON. But why torture ourselves with the past.

(**MYRON** *throws the machine in the wastepaper basket.*)

TILLY. Myron, have you told me everything I should know about the two of you?

MYRON. Look darling, she's dead. What's to be gained?

TILLY. Have you ever considered the possibility that she wasn't the target. That maybe…maybe she simply got in the way of a bullet meant for you.

MYRON. Me?

TILLY. You have to consider the possibility, Myron. Because if it's true, then this night isn't quite over yet.

(**TILLY** *walks over to the curtains and draws them with a sudden dramatic movement. A flash of lightening and a thunder-clap makes* **MYRON** *jump back.*)

TILLY. But now there I go! Like a silly goose putting strange thoughts in your head. You just forget all about it, and go to sleep.

(**TILLY** *heads for the door.*)

MYRON. *(nervously)* Oh honey.

TILLY. Yes.

MYRON. When the police asked where you were tonight…

TILLY. What did I tell them? Why, Darling…they never asked me.

(**TILLY** *exits.* **MYRON** *prepares the couch for bed, climbs in, and turns off the light. The bedroom door slowly opens casting the long shadow of a figure creeping towards the couch. The silhouette of the figure can be seen against the window. It stops just over the couch, raises its arm and strikes downward again and again and again. The light clicks on and standing over by the light switch against the wall is* **MYRON**. *Standing over the couch is* **DENA**.)

MYRON. Ah ha! So it was you!

(**DENA** *jumps back, startled.*)

DENA. Holy Moly, what are you doing there?

MYRON. You mean instead of on the couch?

(**MYRON** *walks up to her.*)

Where if I weren't a light sleeper I'd be a dead one!

DENA. Dead? What, with a rolled up magazine?

(**DENA** *produces a rolled up magazine.*)

There's a mosquito in here. Anyway, I thought you'd be spending the night at Tilly's.

(*Embarrassed,* **MYRON** *walks over to the couch and picks up the magazine.*)

MYRON. Well…do you know what kind of damage you can do with a thing like this? Just look at the size of that advertising supplement. Suppose that had hit me on the head?

DENA. I know, we might have had to spend the rest of the night taking turns combing your hair, the nearest emergency salon miles away, a tourniquet wrapped around your neck keeping precious blood away from your brain where it apparently doesn't do much good anyway! Look, Professor, I saw the look in your eyes when you turned-on the light. You thought I was trying to kill you!

MYRON. I'm sorry. I don't know what to say.

DENA. If I wanted to kill someone I wouldn't use a rolled up magazine with a thick advertising supplement!

MYRON. I know.

DENA. No! I'd use a knife like this!

(**DENA** *materializes a large knife from beneath her nightgown.* **MYRON** *jumps back.*)

DENA. Now, is that so difficult to understand?!

MYRON. *(heart in throat)* No.

DENA. Good! Sometimes I don't know why I bother to stay here!

(**DENA** *storms back into her bedroom slamming the door behind her.*)

MYRON. Ok. It's a cinch I'm not going to get much sleep tonight. Well fine. I'll just move this chair over here and I'll be able to see everything that's happening.

(**MYRON** *drags a large wing chair to a spot in the room strategically located to view both doors. Revealed crouching behind the chair is* **KNUCKLES** *holding a length of piano wire in his hands.* **MYRON** *doesn't notice him as he continues to prepare for the night's long vigil.*)

MYRON. Those three years I spent at Fort Ord are going to come in pretty handy now. I'll be like the night. A shadow to my enemies.

(**MYRON** *moves quietly like a shadow, Never noticing* **KNUCKLES** *is walking up behind him.*)

MYRON. I am a cat. Swift and merciless.

(**MYRON** *now jumps like a cat, only backwards, right into* **KNUCKLES** *path.*)

MYRON. My only weapons are my keen mind, my finely honed senses, and uh…uh…

KNUCKLES. Piano wire?

MYRON. That's good. Piano wire.

(**MYRON** *stops, gulps and turns around and sees* **KNUCKLES** *standing behind him.*)

KNUCKLES. Sure. I saw it in a movie once. It works like this.

(**KNUCKLES** *reaches out his hands holding the length of piano wire and makes a strangling motion and a gurgling sound.* **MYRON** *lets out a shriek, and collapses on the couch, cringing.*)

KNUCKLES. But I can't let you use this one, 'cause its a replacement for my mom's piano.

MYRON. *(jumping up)* Your mom's piano?! You mean you're not going to.?! But…but…but what are you doing in my apartment?!

KNUCKLES. I couldn't sleep. Sometimes when things bother me I just curl up behind a big chair and think.

MYRON. And you just had to pick my chair? After you bought some piano wire for your mother.

KNUCKLES. That's ok, isn't it? What have you got to be worried about anyway. Remember, you're like a rat.

MYRON. That's cat! And never mind!

(**MYRON** *collapses on the couch and* **KNUCKLES** *joins him.*)

KNUCKLES. But I was thinking…

MYRON. This should be good.

KNUCKLES. This Miss Davenport was a reporter, right? Well you still got her tape recorder, right? What if the story she was working on was the thing that got her killed?

MYRON. *(Impressed)* Knuckles, my boy. You sit behind my chair to think anytime you want to. Where did I put that tape recorder? Oh yes!

(**MYRON** *retrieves the recorder out of the wastepaper basket and turns it on.*)

LILAH. *(Off stage voice)* "… And the most recent reports finds Dr. Gibbons not in Africa but in Istanbul: The only city in the world that sits astride two continents – Europe and Asia. A logical place to search for buried fossils. But Istanbul is also the location of the famed Topaki Palace. The ancient citadel where Sultans stored their fabulous treasure. Is it coincidence that a magnificent diamond disappeared the same day as Dr. Gibbons?"

KNUCKLES. Sorry. I guess I wasn't much help.

MYRON. Knuckles, that's it! Don't you see? Lilah Davenport was feeling guilty about something. Somehow she got hold of the diamond. Now listen Knuckles…Knuckles? Say, what's your real name, son?

KNUCKLES. Francis.

MYRON. Now listen, Knuckles, we've got to get this tape to the police.

KNUCKLES. Are you sure you want to?

MYRON. I know what you mean. She's already dead and

it can only serve to mark her as a thief. She apparently stole a diamond that was already stolen by Dr. Gibbons.

KNUCKLES. So where's the diamond now?

MYRON. Where indeed. She came back here. She wanted to say goodbye one last time. No luggage. A handbag with nothing special inside. And her tape recorder.

KNUCKLES. Inside the tape recorder!

(**MYRON** *picks up the tape recorder.*)

MYRON. No. You don't hide something inside something that could also be stolen. Portable jobs like this are expensive. It would catch the eye of any ordinary thief.

KNUCKLES. In her luggage.

MYRON. Same problem. Even if we could find it.

KNUCKLES. She mailed it.

MYRON. She already saw how the mail failed Dr. Gibbons. No, I think we can exclude that too.

KNUCKLES. That only leaves…you.

MYRON. Me?! Why that's brilliant, Knuckles! You're saying to steal and then somehow secretly return the stolen property to the victim until everyone else exhausts themselves searching for it.

KNUCKLES. No, what I said was, "That only leaves…you."

MYRON. Uh, right. But follow me for a second. Why not hide it with a person who didn't know he had it! Who could convincingly deny he ever had it! And being ignorant of it's possession, would even under the most severe torture keep the secret safe!

KNUCKLES. Oh I get ya! They could boil you in oil…

MYRON. Stick bamboo shoots under my fingernails…

KNUCKLES. Place hot coals on your feet…

MYRON. Hang me upside down over a snake pit…

KNUCKLES. Break every one of your bones…

MYRON. *(laughing)* The chumps…they'd get tennis elbow knocking my head against the wall before they'd get anything out of me.

KNUCKLES. *(laughing)* They'd get calluses working you over with them little rubber hoses. They'd...

MYRON. *(stops laughing)* Wait a minute! Wait a minute! We gotta find that diamond! She was already here, waiting for me when I walked into the room, so she had time to hide it. You check the bathroom and I'll start looking in here.

(**KNUCKLES** *exits into the bathroom and* **MYRON** *begins searching around the room. As the elevated train passes, the light it throws off momentarily illuminates a motionless* **FIGURE** *standing outside on the fire-escape, whose silhouette is outlined against the closed drapes.* **MYRON** *grabs a flashlight and quietly exits into the bedroom. The* **FIGURE,** *wearing a ski mask and long overcoat, opens the window and climbs into the room, and quickly hides behind the drapes.* **MYRON** *and* **KNUCKLES** *reenter the room.*)

KNUCKLES. I drew a blank.

MYRON. Me too.

(**MYRON** *leans against the wall near the dingy ornate wall sconce made up of a number of candles and decorative crystals hanging below them.* **KNUCKLES** *stands on the other side of him, perfectly framing the crystal wall sconce between them. There is a special spotlight on the crystal wall sconce accenting its presence.*)

MYRON. It's crystal clear to me that the diamond is here.

KNUCKLES. We know it's not heavy. Which means its very light.

MYRON. No, no. We're up against a wall.

KNUCKLES. If I were just a little brighter.

MYRON. I'm afraid I haven't been very illuminating either.

KNUCKLES. But I can't even hold a candle to you.

MYRON. Wait a minute! Candle...Wall...Light...Crystal. We need to turn on some more lamps to see what we're doing. Follow me to the basement and we'll bring up some more lights.

(**KNUCKLES** *and* **MYRON** *exit and the lone* **FIGURE** *standing behind the drapes, quickly comes out and walks up to the wall sconce. The elevated train passing makes one crystal fall. The* **FIGURE** *picks it up examines it and exits out the back door with it. Seconds later, the* **FIGURE** *backs into the room, hands held high in the air, followed by* **THE FATHER** *holding a gun.)*

THE FATHER. When you elope, ain't it customary to bring along the little woman, professor?

*(***THE FATHER** *takes the crystal.)*

Chickened out at the last second, huh? By the way, this is from a guy whose been there. When you get them a rock this big they're gonna know its a fake.

*(***THE FATHER** *throws the diamond over his shoulder and it goes out the back door. The* **FIGURE** *places its head in its hands.)*

THE FATHER. Ski-mask, huh? Was you gonna run all the way to Canada? Ah, ah, ah. Keep tickling the ceiling with those hands, Professor. I mean you didn't have trouble keeping them busy before with my daughter. And I admit, I was pretty steamed at first. But then I think…Hey, she likes you and what the heck, a professor makes pretty good money, right?

*(***THE FATHER** *looks around the apartment.)*

Well anyway, you're not out on the streets. Now one, we can forget this little unpleasantness and you can get married right away, or two, I can put so many holes in you that I'll be able to play you like a piccolo. Remember, there's advantages to both. If I kill you, you won't have to meet her mother.

(The **FIGURE** *hesitatingly walks toward the bedroom door, prodded by* **THE FATHER** *waving the gun. The* **FIGURE** *quietly opens the door and tiptoes in the bedroom. There is a scream, a thump, and the sound of something falling to the floor.* **DENA** *rushes out.)*

THE FATHER. What happened?

DENA. There's some guy in my room! I conked him good though!

THE FATHER. That wasn't some guy! That was the professor. He's gonna elope with you.

DENA. The professor? Elope with me? Now?

THE FATHER. All I know is he wouldn't even stop long enough to hear me play a John Philip Sousa march.

DENA. Huh?

THE FATHER. But my baby's getting married!

DENA. I'm getting married! Gee, I hope I didn't kill him first.

THE FATHER. Nah! So what do we do now?

DENA. Let's see. I'll need something old...

THE FATHER. The professor.

DENA. Something new...

THE FATHER. The lump on his head.

DENA. Something borrowed...

THE FATHER. Everything in this apartment.

DENA. And something blue.

THE FATHER. Blue? Hmmm...that rock I threw out the door. It's kinda blue.

DENA. Rock?

THE FATHER. Yeah, just not as expensive. I guess he couldn't afford anything better. But his heart was in the right place. You go get it, huh?

DENA. But what about the professor?

THE FATHER. You better let me talk to him first. I don't want him to think that's how newlyweds greet each other in the morning. He might not think that marriage is for him.

(**DENA** *exits.*)

THE FATHER. Com'on Professor. Plenty of time to take a nap later.

(**THE FATHER** *walks into the bedroom. He comes out a second later.*)

THE FATHER. The bum! He skipped out already!

(He gets the gun out of his pocket and exits out the front door. **DENA** *comes in through the back door holding the diamond.)*

DENA. Pop, I got it. Pop?

*(**DENA** puts the diamond in her pocket and **MYRON** walks in carrying a lamp.)*

DENA. Oh, Myron.

*(She rushes into **MYRON**'s arms.)*

MYRON. Myron? Uh…did I wake you?

DENA. Yes, and I'm so sorry.

MYRON. No, no. I'm the one who's sorry.

DENA. But it wasn't your fault. I promise it won't happen again. How's your head?

MYRON. Confused?

DENA. That's only natural.

MYRON. God, I hope not.

DENA. I guess I'll just have to get used to sharing my room with somebody else.

MYRON. There will be nobody else! Not ever!

DENA. Oh yes. I promise.

MYRON. Good!

DENA. But this place. It's not what I imagined. What do you say if I pack a few things.

MYRON. Pack? Oh! Good! Yes, you pack a few things. It's best this way. You know, to get away from here.

*(**MYRON** walks her to the bedroom.)*

I'm going to be making a lot of noise. I'd probably be keeping you up all night long. Neighbors will be complaining about the racket as it is.

DENA. My heart be still…I'll be ready in a few minutes!

*(**DENA** exits into her bedroom.)*

MYRON. Well, at least I'm getting rid of her. That's one good thing.

(**MYRON** *walks over to the front door.*)

MYRON. Knuckles, get up here. Forget those lamps.

(**KNUCKLES** *walks in carrying some lamps.*)

KNUCKLES. What's up?

MYRON. I'm going to drive Dena to the Sleepy Time Motel. We'll get her out of here where it probably isn't safe anyway. Can I borrow some money till tomorrow?

KNUCKLES. Money?! From me?!

MYRON. Just a few bucks. I'll pay you back.

KNUCKLES. I sure miss those carefree days in the park when it was other people that I was borrowing from.

(**KNUCKLES** *hands* **MYRON** *some money, who places it in his pants pocket.* **DENA** *comes out carrying a suitcase.*)

DENA. Aren't you bringing anything.

MYRON. I've got everything I need right here.

(**MYRON** *taps his pants pocket.*)

DENA. Oh my. I'd never thought I'd say this but this is the happiest day of my life.

MYRON. For you and me both.

(*She walks over to* **KNUCKLES** *and hugs him.*)

DENA. It ain't gonna be the same, Knuckles. Next time we see each other I'll be a wife.

(**DENA** *walks out the back door*).

MYRON. Did she say she'd be a wife?

KNUCKLES. I think she said she'd have a knife.

MYRON. How many does she need? You keep looking. I'll be back in a few minutes.

(**MYRON** *exits out the back.* **KNUCKLES** *sits on the couch and casually opens up the book on gynecology lying next to him. He opens it up, thumbs through it quickly, yawns and throws it down and closes his eyes trying to catch a nap. After a moment, his eyes suddenly pop back open and he grabs the book again, and starts slowly looking through it.*)

KNUCKLES. The professor was right! I haven't been giving this course half a chance!

(**TILLY** *enters through the front door, and* **KNUCKLES** *quickly puts the book behind him.*)

TILLY. Where's Myron?

KNUCKLES. He took Dena over to a motel.

TILLY. My Myron?

KNUCKLES. Yeah, but he said he'd only be a few minutes.

TILLY. That's Myron alright.

KNUCKLES. He sure looked happy.

TILLY. Happy? Without me? We'll see about that. Do you know which motel?

KNUCKLES. He told me the name but…I can't remember. I think I'd know it if I saw it though.

TILLY. Come with me and help me find it. We'll take my car.

KNUCKLES. But he said he'd be right back.

TILLY. I can't let Myron go through with it. She could ruin his whole life. And that's not a job for a stranger.

KNUCKLES. Well, ok.

TILLY. Fine. Do you have any gas money I could borrow?

(**KNUCKLES** *reluctantly gives the last of his money to* **TILLY**, *who quickly exits.*)

KNUCKLES. I'm going broke robbing these two people.

(**KNUCKLES** *exits through the front door, carrying his book.* **MYRON** *enters through the back door and goes to a cookie jar on the counter and takes out some money.* **THE FATHER** *enters through the front door.*)

THE FATHER. Got you!

MYRON. What are you talking about?

THE FATHER. So you thought you could skip out on my daughter.

MYRON. Your daughter is downstairs in the car. I'm taking her to the Sleepy Time Motel. I've finally come to my senses.

THE FATHER. Oh. Ooohhh. Oooohhhh! But what are you doing here?

MYRON. If you must know I think I need some more money.

THE FATHER. Why didn't you say so. Hell, here you go.

(**THE FATHER** *puts some money in* **MYRON**'s *pocket and makes him sit down on the couch.* **THE FATHER** *puts his arm around* **MYRON** *who now looks both very confused and uncomfortable.*)

THE FATHER. Anything you want to…you know ask me first?

MYRON. Like what?

THE FATHER. Com'on! You don't gotta be shy. This your first time?

MYRON. No. I've borrowed money lots of times.

THE FATHER. No, no. That's not what I mean. Let me tell you something. Dena looks rough. Come to think of it, she is rough. In fact, sometimes she even scares me. But underneath she's soft…gentle…kinda like a woman. Patience will go a long way with her. I know.

(**MYRON** *fidgets, and* **THE FATHER** *hits him on the side of the ears.*)

THE FATHER. Sit up straight when I'm talking! So anyway, I'm just trying to say, treat her like a lady and be respectful.

MYRON. Ok, ok. You want to join us?

THE FATHER. What did you say?

MYRON. You know, tag along.

THE FATHER. Don't you think I'd be intruding?

MYRON. Intruding? She's your daughter. In fact, you can go without me.

THE FATHER. Go without you? Just me?

MYRON. Hey, we're not talking about putting together a trapeze act. It only takes two, and I'm kind of busy right now.

THE FATHER. *(jumping up)* And that's all marriage means to you? That's what you wanted my money for?

MYRON. *(jumping up)* Marriage?! Marriage?! I don't want to get married! I only wanted this money for her and a motel room!

(**MYRON** *does a take knowing that doesn't sound quite right.*)

THE FATHER. Ya bum ya!

(**THE FATHER** *slugs* **MYRON** *out cold.*)

(*Blackout.*)

End of Scene 2, Act Ii

Scene 3

(AT RISE: **MYRON** *is sitting in a chair tied up and gagged.* **LILAH** *is sitting down in a chair next to him, sipping a martini, with her legs crossed on top of* **MYRON***'s lap.* **MYRON** *neither sees nor hears her.)*

LILAH. Funny, but if Myron and I ever got married this is exactly how I pictured we'd be spending our evenings. Only now Myron is not a willing participant in an intense game of sexual deviation and adventure. No. Myron's danger is real. A victim of his own lack of caution. But if he was muddle-headed I guess I was partly responsible. The diamond drew me like a beacon and I ran aground following its lure, a shipwreck testifying to the greed which can blind any one of us in a moment of weakness. Myron's bad luck was that he tried to follow me, not knowing that I was listing, carrying a cargo full of bilge water as cold and worthless as the pump I owned and called a heart. And as greed had blinded me, love now blinded Myron and he was heading for a particularly nasty rock known as a Fathers Love for his Daughter. A treacherous reef that's capsized more than one stout ship, and since Myron already was going through life bailing water with both hands, one more hole in his hull would mean lights out in a life that was already 50 watts short of a hundred. I could still help him. But he'd have to want me. And only he knew how to reach me.

*(***LILAH*** walks off and ***THE FATHER*** enters from the bedroom carrying some sheets. He goes over to the phone and dials.)*

THE FATHER. Bill, it's me. Get the concrete crew together. Tonight we pour. I don't care if you heard I was going back to school! Really? A PTA bake sale tonight? No, no. Not important. You just get that crew together now! Ok, ok, on the way back we'll pick up some cream-puffs. No. I don't want any lady-fingers.

(He removes a large butcher knife from his belt.)

THE FATHER. *(cont'd)* The idea of naming a pastry like it was once some part of the human anatomy makes me queasy.

*(**THE FATHER** hangs up the phone and feels the edge of the knife.)*

You should appreciate this, Professor. Thousands of years from now some paleontologist of the future will find you, knock all that concrete off you, put you back together and make you an exhibit in a museum. Maybe they'll pose you looking through a microscope. Or maybe fix you so you're looking up at the stars. However you'll end up, one things for certain. It won't be with your arm around my daughter.

*(As **MYRON** struggles, **THE FATHER** lays the sheets down and measures **MYRON**'s dimensions with a tape measure.)*

'Course maybe I was too strict in raising her. Sometimes I think she was afraid to bring boyfriends over to the house.

*(**THE FATHER** puts the knife down and sits down my **MYRON**, and takes out his wallet, sometimes showing him pictures.)*

Gosh, she was a cute kid. My little girl. Only not so little now.

*(**THE FATHER** turns on the radio and removes a gun from his back pocket and points it at **MYRON**.)*

But you already know that, don't you, Professor? Well I guess this is it. I don't think I forgot anything.

*(**DENA** bursts through the back door.)*

DENA. Pop!

THE FATHER. Except my daughter who's been waiting in the car. Doggoneit!

DENA. What are you doing to the professor?

THE FATHER. Oh uh...we're rehearsing a ventriloquist act for the wedding reception. See, the professor is gagged but he can still make his voice come out of my mouth. Watch.

(**THE FATHER** *sits on the professor's lap and speaks in a high pitched voice.*)

Go away, Dena, I'm busy now.

(*Normal voice.*)

Cute, huh?

DENA. Why is he tied up?

THE FATHER. Part of the show. He's an escape artist too, like the great Houdini.

DENA. And the sheets?

THE FATHER. We close with a magic act. That's how he disappears.

DENA. And the gun?

THE FATHER. For the critics, in case the reviews are bad.

DENA. You'll need more bullets.

THE FATHER. I really am busy honey...

DENA. Pop, I got one last question? Why do you want to kill the professor.

THE FATHER. Ok, ok! Yes, I'm gonna kill him! Because he's running out on the marriage.

DENA. You know I don't want to force anybody to marry me.

THE FATHER. But he dishonored you!

DENA. No Pop. Not the professor.

THE FATHER. Well...can I shoot him on general principle? I mean look at this place!

DENA. Pop.

THE FATHER. Ok, ok.

DENA. Shouldn't we untie the professor now?

THE FATHER. It's up to you. But remember I was going to kill him. Some people could overreact to a thing like that.

DENA. I guess we could give him a chance to cool down. Goodbye, Professor, thanks for everything.

(**DENA** *kisses him on the forehead.*)

THE FATHER. So where do we go from here?

(**DENA** *and* **THE FATHER** *walk out towards the front door arm and arm.*)

DENA. Back to where we were, I guess. You'll be my pop. The guy that's always cared for me and always will.

THE FATHER. Awwww, Dena...

(**DENA** *hits him on the side of the head.*)

DENA. Hey, stand up straight when I'm talking to you... Father.

(**THE FATHER** *and* **DENA** *hug.* **MYRON** *just rolls his eyes and shakes his head.*)

DENA. Oh, by the way professor, I guess you can take this back to.

(**DENA** *removes the diamond from her pocket and lays it on the table.* **MYRON** *eyes become round as saucers as He recognizes it as a diamond.*)

THE FATHER. Do you believe how cheap he was. I say we flush the worthless thing down the toilet, before he tries to fool anybody else with it.

(**THE FATHER** *picks up the diamond and heads for the bathroom.* **TILLY** *enters through the front door. She sees* **MYRON** *tied up. She also sees* **THE FATHER** *holding the diamond. She runs in front of him blocking his path.*)

TILLY. Wait! What are you doing?

THE FATHER. Don't worry, Lady, everything's fine. Just family business. Who are you?

DENA. Let me introduce you to Tilly's Plumms.

THE FATHER. I see!

TILLY. That's *Tilly* Plumms.

THE FATHER. Oh. Say you got blood on your head.

TILLY. I bumped it getting out of the car. Now why is Myron tied up? Who are you? And what is that you're holding?

THE FATHER. I'm Dena's father. And this is a poor excuse of an engagement present that this bum was going to try to give my daughter. I'm going to get rid of it.

TILLY. Oh, Myron. How could you. You've hurt so many people. Pretending you loved them, only to run out on them later.

THE FATHER. You too, huh? Boy he sure got a lot of mileage out of this piece of glass.

TILLY. Here give it to me. I'll drop it down the deepest well where it can't hurt anybody anymore.

THE FATHER. Sure. I understand.

DENA. Don't give it too her, Pop.

THE FATHER. What?

DENA. When she came in. She didn't go straight to the professor. She went straight to you. Or should I say, straight to the rock you were carrying.

TILLY. No!

(**DENA** *walks up to* **MYRON** *and looks at his head.*)

DENA. True, the professor may not have the best head in the world on his shoulders, but at least it's smooth as a baby's bottom. Now before you start making up your own jokes you should know there's not a lump on it. Yet Tilly's head is bleeding just at the spot where I hit the person who entered my room.

THE FATHER. Then it wasn't the professor I found trying to sneak out this evening. And that rock he held...

DENA. ...Was an actual diamond. The one Dr. Gibbons must have sent to the professor. Which Tilly must have found and come back here to retrieve after you threw it downstairs.

TILLY. *(takes out a gun)* Alright. It *was* me. I came back here to kill Myron when I found out he was trying to keep it a secret from me. But only after I figured out you were in love with him, too. Only I killed the reporter by mistake. But I didn't care about that either. Because I knew she was also falling in love with Myron.

(**THE FATHER** *leans over to a still bound and gagged* **MYRON** *and whispers.*)

THE FATHER. Hey pal, you're doing ok! How long does it take to become one of these paleontologist type fellows?

TILLY. Longer than you got time left, pop. I knew I'd be the last to blame for any deaths as long as Dr. Gibbons remained at large.

DENA. But what if the police have already collared him? Are you certain you've still got a patsy to pin it on? Are you really sure Dr. Gibbons is still on the loose?

(*The radio* **ANNOUNCER** *interrupts the music that has been playing.*)

ANNOUNCER. Flash! Dr. Gibbons is still on the loose. The public is advised to continue to take extra precautions until he is captured. We now return you to your listening pleasure.

TILLY. I'm sure. In fact, maybe he's on his way here now. Maybe he'll be on one of those elevated trains that comes by. I only wish he would come. It might help throw the police off the track for what has to happen next and I'll be sitting pretty.

(**THE FATHER**, *unseen by* **TILLY**, *slowly removes the meat cleaver from his back pocket, raises it and takes a step towards* **TILLY** *as she turns around and sees him.*)

TILLY. *(Continued)* And I don't need a trim.

(**THE FATHER** *laughs nervously and drops the meat clever.*)

TILLY. Thanks.

(*The sound of an elevated train approaching is heard.* **MYRON** *tries to make himself heard beneath the gag.* **TILLY** *takes it off.*)

TILLY. What is it Myron?

MYRON. I've been thinking about this children thing we were talking about earlier. I think you should have as many as you'd like.

TILLY. Ok, Myron, I will. Just promise me you won't be too mad if I have them with somebody else.

DENA. You're going to shoot us?

TILLY. Why not? Like everything else in life, murder's easier the second time around. You shouldn't have hurt me, Myron.

THE FATHER. Thanks a lot, Myron!

DENA. Just a second. You forgot about Knuckles.

TILLY. It's hard to forget about a guy who's curled up behind the back seat of my car with his head buried inside a book.

DENA. A book?

(**DENA** *looks at the couch and notices the book on gynecology is gone.*)

Oh. That book.

MYRON. Really? A book? Knuckles? Well, if I'm going to die at least I have the satisfaction of knowing I've finally reached a student. Just think, a whole new world is going to spread open before him. He's finally sticking his nose into something that's worth sticking into. He'll spend many happy hours losing himself inside something well, that I've never wanted to leave. He'll finally be able to lick…

DENA. PROFESSOR STOP!

MYRON. What?

DENA. Can we just change the subject?

TILLY. Yes. Like to your imminent deaths. And the fact that maybe I'll be able to use to my advantage the fact that Knuckles is downstairs by himself in my car with no alibi.

MYRON. Ah ha! In other words make the police think that Knuckles had cracked!

TILLY. Just for that Myron, I'm going to shoot you first. Any last words?

MYRON. *(pause)* Want a peanut?

TILLY. You're a cool one, Myron. But I can be just as cool as you. Sure, I'll have peanut.

DENA. Over there.

*(**DENA** motions to the jar labeled "Peanuts" containing Stingy, the scorpion. **TILLY** walks over and grabs the jar.)*

TILLY. Just to prove to you I can be as emotionless towards you as you've been towards me.

MYRON. A lesson I deserve. Help yourself.

*(Before **TILLY** can unscrew the top of the jar, **KNUCKLES** walks in with his head buried inside a book. Without looking up, he grabs a soft drink off the desk, a bag of chips off the end table and the jar out of **TILLY**'s hand)*

KNUCKLES. Be in the car.

*(**KNUCKLES** exits)*

MYRON. Just one last thing. Could you forget about trying to pin this thing on Knuckles and just shoot him now? And can I watch?

TILLY. This is going to be easier than I thought. As for the rest of you…This train coming by will do a lot to drown out the sound of gunfire. Goodbye all. I wish I could say, I'll miss you. But I haven't missed yet.

*(As the elevated train roars by, it illuminates a **FIGURE** standing on the fire-escape. He can be seen pointing his gun at **TILLY**. The lights fade and a volley of gunfire is heard)*

(Blackout.)

End of Scene 3, Act Ii

Scene 4

*(**SETTING:** Bare. Black.)*

*(**AT RISE:** Spotlight on **LILAH DAVENPORT** in a business suit. Her pace is slow and measured. She is holding a portable tape recorder. She walks forward and stops. A light comes on illuminating **MYRON** who is standing next to her. Only his face is visible. It is a happy face. She makes her observation about him into the recorder. He neither sees nor hears her.)*

LILAH. Myron Amberworth. 34 years of age, 5'11," 170 lbs. A professor of Comparative Paleontology. Now involved in of one of the State's largest excavations.

*(The lights widen to show **MYRON** wearing a striped prisoners shirt and a ball and chain attached to his ankle. He is carefully breaking open a small rock with his sledge hammer, examining what is inside.)*

LILAH. What was he guilty of? Complicity in theft. But only confessing to the charge as a way to pursue his studies in peace and quiet. When the State eventually realized their mistake he was released.

*(The lights dim on **MYRON** but continues to follow **LILAH** as she walks up toward the audience.)*

And what about me. Where I am, no Governor's pardon can reach. I don't know what drew me to Myron in the first place. Frankly I'd seen better muscles in a bowl of bouillabaisse and he was shorter than a Hollywood marriage. But he was an original, and to a kid like me who lived on the hand-me-downs from her older sisters, that meant quite a lot. He didn't quite fit and I might be embarrassed to be seen at a nice party with him draped over my shoulders. But he made me feel warm inside, and he was easy to keep clean. *(pause)* And there's one thing I know. If you don't ask for too much more from either your man or your coat, odds are you won't be too disappointed whichever one you lose. You go on. Like I've got to go on now.

(She walks along the edge of the stage)

LILAH. *(cont'd)* Oh yes. What happened to Tilly? She was killed by Dr. Gibbons before she could kill again. I only add that parenthetically because this was never about Dr. Gibbons or Tilly or even about the theft of a diamond whose storied legend of a curse grew by yet another chapter written in blood. This was about me and a reporter's instinct to set the record straight. A case in which one of the villains became one of the victims. Who had angled hard for byline in a story that will never go to press...in a place that has never had a newspaper. Brother! If I weren't already overflowing to the gills in formaldehyde, I'd really need a drink.

(She turns to walk away, but stops and turns back towards the audience.)

Oh by the way, that wasn't a diamond Tilly took off the wall sconce and died for. It was just another cheap fifty cent crystal, shinier than the rest perhaps but no more valuable. The diamond is still there. Inside a room that's now for rent. So the next time any of you are a little down on your luck, and you're forced to rent a furnished apartment in a part of town that looks like a future address for a wrecking ball, don't despair. If your forced to drink cheap booze out of an old mayonnaise jar, take heart. And if Saturday night entertainment involves watching a race between two undernourished cockroaches on a dinning room carpet that's got more spots on it than a litter of Dalmatians, don't panic. Help just might be closer than you think. Good night and good luck.

*(**LILAH** walks off stage as the lights fade.)*

End of Play

PROPERTY PLOT

PRESET

Box with shoulder bag (by desk)
Envelopes one pink (on desk)
Towel (on couch)
Small stereo radio (on bookshelf)
Silver candlestick (on round table)
Small pile of bones (on desk)
Magnifying glass (on desk)
Calipers (on desk)
Bag of fast food takeout (on coffee table)
Fortune cookie (on coffee table)
Bottle of liquor and glasses (on bookshelf)
Paperweight (on bookshelf)
Phone (on desk)
Pop bottle (on coffee table)
Bag of chips (on round table)
Portrait of Tilly and Myron (on wall)

PROP TABLE

Portable tape recorder (Lilah)
Tattered briefcase with large bone inside (Myron)
Wallet with $20 inside (Myron)
Pocket watch (Father)
Gun (Father)
Can with coiled snakes that jump out (Father)
Large jar labeled "Peanuts" (Father)
Folded up paper (Knuckles)
Large boulder (Knuckles)
Steering wheel (Knuckles)
Comic book (Knuckles)
Car keys (Lilah)
Small plain wrapped package with large diamond inside (Tilly)
Telegram (Dena, delivered to her at front door)
Lipstick and compact (Dena)
Rolled up magazine (Dena)
Knife (Dena)
Piano wire (Knuckles)
A few dollar bills (Knuckles)
Suitcase (Dena)
A few dollar bills (Father)

Large met cleaver (Father)
Large medical text (Father)
Gun (Tilly)

COSTUME PLOT

DR. MYRON AMBERWORTH: White shirt with simple tweed suit, bow tie, sweater vest, horn rimmed glasses. Later, Bermuda shorts and beach sandals, sunglasses and towel. Lastly, a stripped prisoner's outfit with ball and chain and small sledge hammer.

TILLY PLUMMS: Blouse, pleated skirt, high heels, purse to match and earrings. Later, black nylon suit, trench coat, ski mask, black rubber rain boots, black gloves and fedora.

LILAH DAVENPORT: Black sexy, sultry dress and high heels.

DENA: Blue faded cut off jeans, t-shirt, leather or denim jacket with image of scorpion on back (though looks more like lobster), worn out tennis shoes, hair simple over eyes. Later, plain skirt and blouse, white shoes, hair done up in pony tail with large ribbon in shape of butterfly. Lastly, oversize men's pajamas.

KNUCKLES. Blue faded cut off jeans, t-shit, leather or denim jacket with image of scorpion on back (though looks more like lobster), worn out tennis shoes.

FATHER: Jean Overalls, red long sleeve shirt, hard hat and work boots. Later, ski mask and raincoat. Lastly, fireman's outfit with oxygen mask.

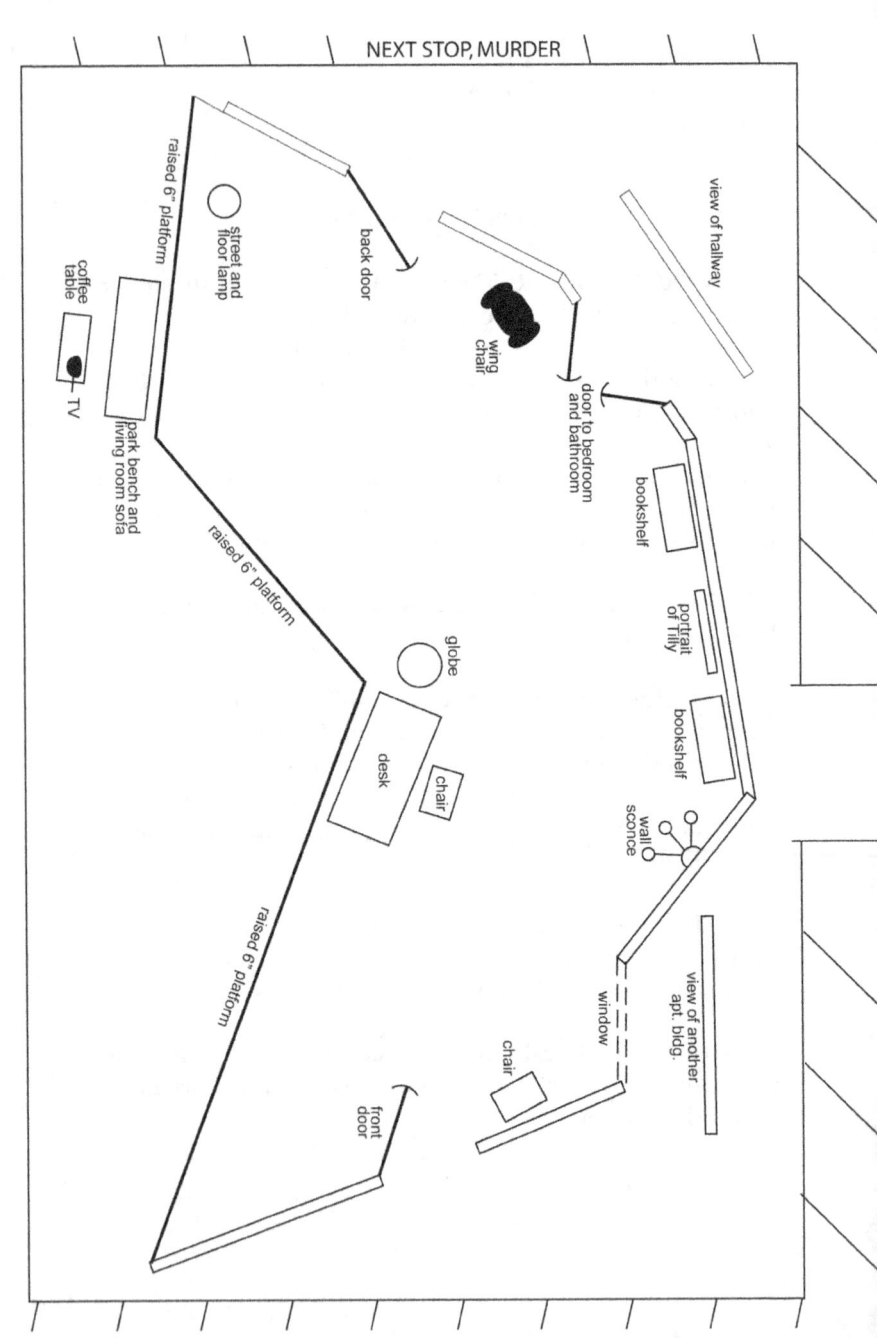

From the Reviews of
NEXT STOP, MURDER...

"Harkens back to the classic fast and sassy film noir style. The script is smart."
- *The Tolucan Times*

"Deliciously Noir."
- *Studio City Sun*

Also by
Frank Semerano...

Kaputnik

Murder Me Once

The Tangled Snarl

Thataway Jack

A Vampire Reflects

Please visit our website **samuelfrench.com** for complete
descriptions and licensing information

OTHER TITLES AVAILABLE FROM SAMUEL FRENCH

A VERY MERRY UNAUTHORIZED CHILDREN'S SCIENTOLOGY PAGEANT
Kyle Jarrow

Musical / 5m, 5f (Doubling possible) / Interior

A jubilant cast of children celebrate the controversial religion in uplifting pageantry and song. The actual teachings of The Church of Scientology are explained and dissected against the candy-colored backdrop of a traditional nativity play. Pageant is a musical biography of the life of L. Ron Hubbard, with child-friendly explanations of Hubbard's notion of the divided mind (embodied by the lovely identical twins Emma and Sophie Whitfield in matching brain outfits) and a device called the e-meter (or electropsychometer), used to monitor the human psyche, which is demonstrated by stick puppets. Grade school children, portraying Tom Cruise, Kirstie Alley, John Travolta, and other less starry Scientologists, brings the controversial Church of Scientology to jubilant life in story and song.

SAMUELFRENCH.COM

www.ingramcontent.com/pod-product-compliance
Lightning Source LLC
Chambersburg PA
CBHW070646300426
44111CB00013B/2288